MOTHERHOOD IN ISLAM

MOTHERHOOD IN ISLAM

Aliah Schleifer

The Islamic Texts Society–USA

With appreciation and thanks to the Louisville Islamic Center.

ISBN 1-887752-01-3

Printed in USA

The Islamic Texts Society–USA
Mockingbird Valley
Louisville, Kentucky 40207
Phone/fax 502-897-3641; 502-893-7373
email: grayh101@aol.com

بسم الله الرحمن الرحيم

AL-AZHAR ISLAMIC RESEARCH ACADEMY GENERAL DEPARTMENT For Research, Writting & Translation	الأزهر مجمع البحوث الاسلامية الادارة العامة للبحوث والتأليف والترجمة

السيد الأستاذ/ عبد الله شليفر

السلام عليكم ورحمة الله وبركاته وبعد

فبناء على الطلب المقدم منكم بشأن فحص كتاب "الأمومة في الإسلام" (باللغة الإنجليزية) تأليف الأستاذة عالية شليفر.

نفيد بأن الكتاب المذكور يحتوى على معلومات جيدة حول مكانة الأم في الشريعة الإسلامية يمكن الاستفادة منها لمتكلمي اللغة الإنجليزية ولا مانع من طبعه ونشره.

والله الموفق،،

والسلام عليكم ورحمة الله وبركاته،،

أسامة قناوي

مدير عام
الإدارة العامة للبحوث والتأليف والترجمة

تحريرا في ١٦ من صفر ١٤٠٧ هـ
الموافق ٢٠/١٠/١٩٨٦

APPROVAL OF THE TEXT MOTHERHOOD IN ISLAM BY ALIAH SCHLEIFER ISSUED BY THE ISLAMIC RESEARCH ACADEMY OF AL-AZHAR.

ACKNOWLEDGEMENTS

I would like to thank Dr. Ghunaim for his direction and guidance, and my husband and colleagues in the E.L.I. for their encouragement.

بســم ٱلله الرحمٰن الرحيم

وصلّى ٱلله على سيدنا محمّد وعلى آله وأصحابه أجمعين

DEDICATION

This book is dedicated to my parents and my children.

TABLE OF CONTENTS

Page

PART I. THE PERSPECTIVE OF THE CHILD
TOWARDS THE MOTHER

Chapter

PART II. THE PERSPECTIVE OF THE MOTHER
TOWARDS THE CHILD

PART III. THE PERSPECTIVE OF FATHER AND
MOTHER IN CASE OF DIVORCE

FOREWORD

I

In all the issues that she deals with, Aliah Schleifer has resorted to the basic, steadfast and most reliable sources of Islam, namely, the Qur'ān and the Ḥadīths. To explain meanings she has resorted to numerous classic sources. It is therefore, with utmost pleasure and pride that I present to readers of English this valuable research in the hope that it will enlighten them on the status of women in Islam, a subject which has long been misunderstood and inaccurately treated. I hope to see this book translated into other languages besides English.

Sincere thanks are due to the author for the pains she has taken in referring to numerous original Arabic sources and carefully selecting and further elucidating the pertinent examples and evidence she has chosen to cite.

May God Almighty make her work beneficial to others and reward her for it.

Sheikh Abdul Galil Shalaby
Former Secretary General,
The Academy of Islamic Research,
Al-Azhar.

FOREWORD

II

The reader of recent religious studies often observes with deep regret that most of these works are dominated by subjective thinking on the part of the researchers. In the end such studies seem more to be expressions of a point-of-view than of objective study.

But this thorough study undertaken by Aliah Schleifer leaves us little room but to register our deep appreciation for the accurate and intellectually objective path that she has charted.

She is committed to presenting with utmost accuracy the exact Qur'ānic verses, Prophetic Sunnah and the orthodox interpretation and elaborations. And she has displayed great concern in checking the authenticity, accuracy and correctness of the Ḥadīth.

The reader feels quite secure; certain he is treading on the firm ground of trustworthy scholarship.

Aliah Schleifer compiles one accurate text after another until she reaches a conclusive insight about motherhood in Islam. That conclusion rests upon a very firm pillar of exact texts from the mainstream of Islam.

We look forward with great expectations to Aliah Schleifer's future work.

Prof. Aḥmed Ghunaim
Prof. of Islamic Studies,
American University in Cairo,
Member, Tafsir Committee of Al-Azhar.

FOREWORD

III

I was pleased to read this serious study based on precise, objective research undertaken by the American Muslim, Mrs. Aliah Schleifer, on *Motherhood in Islam.* It is a call for basing the family entity and childrearing on the tenets of Islam - an entity which does not have materialism and conflict as its goal, but rather is a response to Allah's injunction as manifested in the Qur'ān and Ḥadīth. *Motherhood in Islam* emphasizes the qualities of the perfect Muslim mother and the requirement to respect her. It also encourages mothers of the future to give more care to childrearing for the benefit of future generations and for society as a whole.

As the world community is currently in a state of conflict - a state in which egotism reigns, it is in dire need of the models of motherhood which appear in *Motherhood in Islam*. Sacrifice, affection and self-denial are presented by the author as being an extension of the mercy of Islam. It becomes clear that the Islam referred to, which is based on original sources - the Qur'ān, the Sunnah and their application - differs from what is practised nowadays by many Muslims. In fact *Motherhood in Islam* can benefit all people who are trying to cultivate the good in themselves, their families and their community.

Ibrahim Mohammed Al-Battawy,
Former Prof. of Al-Azhar University.

Transliteration

Arabic Letter	Transliteration
ء	ʼ
ب	b
ت	t
ث	th
ج	j
ح	ḥ
خ	kh
د	d
ذ	dh
ر	r
ز	z
س	s
ش	sh
ص	ṣ
ض	ḍ
ط	ṭ
ظ	ẓ
ع	ʻ
غ	gh
ف	f
ق	q
ك	k
ل	l
م	m
ن	n
و	w
ه	h
ة	t
ي	y

Short Vowels

ـَ	a
ـُ	u
ـِ	i

Long Vowels

ـَا	ā
ـُو	ū
ـِي	ī

Diphthongs

ـَوْ	aw
ـَيْ	ay
ـِيّ	iyy
ـُوّ	uww

INTRODUCTION

It is the author's hope that this book will provide an English-speaking audience with a fuller understanding of the bases for the concept of motherhood in Islam as found in the Qur'ān, Ḥadīth and *fiqh* (Islamic jurisprudence). It is further hoped that in doing so this book will fulfil the contemporary need for delineation of the role of the mother in Islam and its importance. Fatima Hereen has observed that although family life was traditionally seen as being "human nature", the various "isms", "modernism", "socialism", etc. have attempted to turn values upside down and eliminate the concept of matrimonial life.[1]

There is, however, a lack of published works, in both English and Arabic, focussing on motherhood in Islam, despite the current general interest in all aspects of women's status in Islam. The published works contain limited discussions within broader categories, e.g. the family or women in Islam. Even this limited discussion is more readily found in Arabic than it is in English.

Generally, more has been written about the contemporary Muslim woman and society, often contrasting her life with that of Western women, rather than investigating the formal Islamic bases of her status. Quite frequently, such discussions are rebuttals of local life styles, thus representing behaviours which arise from a merge of "cultural tradition" and one of the legal schools of Islam, i.e., Mālikī, Shāfi'ī, Ḥānafī or Ḥanbalī, according to the country of the author, rather than representing a comparative overview of the four schools.

Nevertheless certain valuable insights about the nature and importance of motherhood in Islam do emerge from the published literature. Dr. Aḥmad Ghunaim, for example, demonstrates that the Islamic concept of motherhood is not one of punishment, but rather that of the martyr.[2] First, he shows how the terminology, which is used to describe pregnancy and childbirth is the same used to describe the one who goes to fight *jihād,* i.e.(كُرْه)[3]. He then illustrates how considering the mother a martyr(شهيدة)thus places her in the highest of categories with respect to Allah's blessings. He refers to:

Sūrah 4: Verse 69

« الّذين أنْعَمَ آلله عَلَيْهِمْ مِنَ النَّبِيّنَ والِصّدّيقينَ والشُّهَداءِ وَالصَّالحينَ وَحَسُنَ أُولٰئِكَ رفيقًا » .

> "... those unto whom Allah has shown favour, of the Prophets, and the sincere (the lovers of truth), and the martyrs (those who testify) and the righteous. The best of company are they."

Then he mentions a Ḥadīth which includes the woman who dies in childbirth as one of the martyrs, plus other related Ḥadīths.[4] Ghunaim thereby stresses the difference between a woman who faces childbirth as a punishment for "original" sin and the Muslim woman who sees it as a chance to face pain and the danger of a martyr for the sake of Allah.[5]

Another insight was made by Dr. 'Abdel 'Aziz Kamel in a paper presented at the International Conference in Cairo. Dr. Kamel, referring to the Muslim mother early in the history of Islam, describes how, in Madina, the mother sought knowledge for herself and her child. She used her knowledge in her daily life, in caring for the generation in which she lived and the generation she prepared for the future. In such a society, he says, rights came after obligations, and giving was more important than taking.[6]

Ḥammūdah 'Abd Al-'Āṭī makes the important point that although the ultimate responsibility of both parent and child is to Allah, this does not invalidate the principles of inter-generational concern, kindness and mutual obligation, especially in matters of subsistence and general care.[7]

'Abd Al-'Āṭī's book is a useful, comprehensive work, covering all aspects of the family in Islam. Throughout the book, he attempts to give the Islamic perspective, while making comparisons with Christianity and Judiasm, and in some instances, with early Roman law and pre-Islamic practices.

Motherhood in Islam, however, is but an attempt to see the subject for itself, i.e., to elucidate the actual bases in Islam for the concept of motherhood. Rather than making comparisons with alien concepts, Islam is left to speak for itself. The basic sources referred to are: (1) the Qur'ān, as it is the primary source of Islamic concepts and regulations. Reference is made to all passages concerning the mother. For explication of these verses, reference is made to the *tafāsīr* of Aṭ-Ṭabarī (3rd-4th cent. Heg.), Al-Qurṭubī (7th cent. Heg.) and Ibn Kathīr (8th cent. Heg.), thus, providing an overview of classical exegeses, which include *fiqh* representing the schools of opinion existing at that time and juridical rulings. (2) Ḥadīth concerning motherhood in Islam are central to the book, and the standard reputable collections are referred to, as well as those found in the *tafāsīr,* if well narrated. Emphasis is given to the *Ṣaḥīḥain* of Al-Bukhārī and Muslim. Exegeses from the classical period, as well as judicial rulings serve to clarify the Ḥadīths.

NOTES

[1]Aisha Lemu and Fatima Hereen, ***Woman in Islam*** (England: Derbyshire Print) 1976/1396, p. 33.

[2]Aḥmad Ghunaim, *Al-Mar'ah Mundhu An-Nasha'a Baina At-Tajrīm Wa At-Takrīm* (Cairo: Al-Kailanī) 1980/1401, p. 139.

[3]Ibid., p. 141; Sūrah 46, Verse 15: « حَمَلَتْهُ أُمُّهُ كُرْهاً وَوَضَعَتْهُ كُرْهاً » .
"... His mother beareth him with reluctance, and bringeth him forth with reluctance,...",
and Sūrah 2, Verse 216: « كُتِبَ عليكمْ القتالُ وهُوَ كُرْهٌ لكمْ » .
"Warfare is ordained for you, though it is hateful unto you ..."; (كُرْه) is something done under compulsion that one would not ordinarily do willingly, i.e., one does it for the sake of Allah.

[4]Muḥammad Khān, *Ḥusn al-Uswah Bimā Thābit Min Allāh Wa Rasūlihi Fī An-Niswa* (Beirut: Mu'assasah Ar-Risālah) Bāb Mā Warada Fī Shahādat An-Nafsā' Wa Makāniha 'Alā Al-Mautā, p. 493.

« وعن عبادة بن الصامت فى حديث طويل يرفعه (وفى النفساء يقتلها وولدها جمعا شهادة) » .

"Narrated 'Ubādah Ibn Aṣ-Ṣāmit (in a longer version of the Ḥadīth): A woman who dies in childbirth together with the baby becomes a martyr." (Aḥmad and Aṭ-Ṭabarānī).

[5]Ghunaim, p. 144.

[6]Dr. 'Abdel 'Aziz Kamel, "The Role of Woman in the Building of the First Islamic Society", *International Islamic Conference in Cairo, 1975* (Centre for Population Studies and Research: Al-Azhar Univ.), 1975, p. 27.

[7]Ḥammūdah 'Abd Al-'Āṭī, *The Family Structure in Islam* (American Trust Publications), 1977, p. 183.

PART I

THE PERSPECTIVE OF THE CHILD TOWARDS THE MOTHER

CHAPTER I

REVERENCE FOR AND GOOD TREATMENT OF THE MOTHER

The relationship of the Muslim to his parents should be of the highest order of human relationships. This includes spiritual, financial and emotional responsibilities, and is on-going, even beyond the point of death. Ordinances are defined in the Qur'ān relating to this point, and are further specified by Ḥadīth, *fiqh* and commentary. The reward for satisfactory compliance with the Qur'ānic ordinances is Paradise:

« عن معاوية بن جاهمة أن جاهمة جاء إلى النبى ﷺ فقال : يارسول آلله أردت أن أغزو وقد جئت أستشيرك ؟ فقال : هل لك من أم ؟ قال نعم ، قال : فالزمها فإن الجنة عند رجلها » .

> "Narrated Mu'āwiyyah Ibn Jāhmah that Jāhmah (رضى) went to the Prophet (ﷺ) and said: O Messenger of Allah (ﷺ), I want to fight and I have come to ask your advice. He said: Do you have a mother? Jāhmah said: Yes. He said: Then, stay with her because Paradise is under her foot." (An-Nasā'ī, Ibn Mājah, Al-Ḥākim and Aṭ-Ṭabarānī)[1]

> هما جنتُكَ ونارُكَ – يعنى الوالدين (ابن ماجة – عن أبى أمامة) .

> "Narrated Abū Umāmah: They are your Paradise and your Hell-fire" – i.e., the parents. (Ibn Mājah)[2]

Thus, the clarification of these ordinances becomes essential to the Muslim, who wishes to know exactly how he can attain this reward, and exactly what will block him from it. In general, most statements of responsibility to parents include both father and mother, but the mother, in Islam, is granted more in this respect:

« حدثنا قُتَيبةُ بنُ سعيدٍ : حدثنا جريرٌ ، عن عُمارةَ بن القعقاع بن شُبْرُمَة ، عن أبى زُرْعة عن أبى هُريرة رضى آلله عنهُ قال : جاءَ رجلٌ إلى رسول آلله ﷺ فقال : يارسول آلله مَنْ أحقُّ الناس بُحسْنِ صحابتى ؟ قال : أمُّكَ ، قال : ثمّ مَنْ ؟ قال : أمُّكَ ، قال : ثمّ مَنْ ؟ قال : أمُّكَ ، قال : ثمّ مَنْ ؟ قال : ثمّ أبوك .

وقال ابن شُبْرُمة ويحيى بن أيُّوب : حدثنا أبو زرعة مثله .

> "Narrated Abū Hurairah (رضى): A man came to Allah's Apostle (ﷺ) and said, 'O Apostle of Allah! Who is more entitled to be treated with the best companionship by me?' The Prophet (ﷺ) said, 'Your mother.' The man said, 'Then who?' The Prophet (ﷺ) said, 'Your mother.' The man further said, 'Then who?' The Prophet (ﷺ) said, 'Your mother.' The man said again, 'Then who?' The Prophet (ﷺ) said, 'Then your father.'" (Al-Bukhārī and Muslim)[3]

An-Nawawī says that « الصحابة » here means *companionship,* and is intended to urge one towards kindness to relatives, the most deserving of whom is the mother and then the father. Giving the opinion of the *'Ulamā'* (the Muslim scholars), he says that the reason for giving the mother preference is due to her exhausting efforts for the sake of her child, her compassion, her service, the great difficulty of pregnancy, delivery, nursing and rearing of the child, her service and care for the child when it is sick, etc. In the view of the *'Ulamā',* the mother is the strongest member of the family in kindness and devotedness.[4]

There are two verses in the Qur'ān, which provide general injunction on the believers to good treatment of parents. The first is:

> "Worship none save Allah (only), and be good to parents." (2:83)

In their commentary on this verse, Aṭ-Ṭabarī, Ibn Kathīr and Al-Qurṭubī are in agreement about the meaning of « إحساناً » (usually translated as "to be good to"), but Ibn Kathīr devotes more discussion to good speech towards parents, while both Al-Qurṭubī and Ibn Kathīr stress parents' rights.

At-Ṭabarī states that grammatically, the expression « وَبالوالِدَيْن إحسَانا » is connected to (معطوف على) the preceding one « لَا تَعْبُدُونَ إِلَّا آللهَ » and thus the meaning is connected.[5] Speaking of the two connected expressions, Ibn Kathīr says that these are the highest and greatest of the rights, i.e., the right of Allah, the Most Blessed and the Most High, that He be worshipped alone, with nothing associated with Him; then, after that, is the right of His creatures, and He firmly commissions them and their children with the right of parents, and thus Allah draws a parallel between His right and the right of parents.[6] Al-Qurṭubī says that Allah, the Great and Lofty, makes a parallel in this verse, between the right of parents and the Unity (of Allah) because the first formation (genesis) proceeds from Allah, and the second formation – up-bringing – proceeds from the parents. Thus, Allah compares thankfulness to parents with thankfulness to Him; this being expressed explicitly in Sūrah 31, Verse 14: "Give thanks unto Me and unto thy parents."[7]

By way of explanation of the meaning of « إحسانا », Aṭ-Ṭabarī says it is to show kindness to parents, courteous speech, the lowering of the wing of submission as a mercy to them, tenderness, compassion, prayer for good to come to them and other similar deeds. Al-Qurṭubī reiterates this definition, adding that the believers should keep up relationships with the people their parents love.[8] To explain the meaning of « إحسانا », Ibn Kathīr refers to Al-Ḥasan Al-Baṣrī's definition of another form of the word « حُسْناً », which is also found in Sūrah 2, Verse 83. Al-Baṣrī defines « حُسْناً » with reference to speech as such speech "that commands kindness, terminates objectionable remarks, and is gentle, and restrains one and pardons."[9] To further clarify his definition, Ibn Kathīr quotes the following Ḥadīth:

« قال الإمام أحمد : حدثنا روح حدثنا أبو عامر الخراز عن أبى عمران الجونى عن عبد آلله بن الصامت عن أبى ذر رضى آلله عنهُ عن النبى ﷺ أنه قال : لا تحقرن من المعروف شيئا وإن لم تجد فالق أخاك بوجه متطلق واخرجه مسلم

فى صحيحه والترمزى وصححه من حديث أبى عامر الخراز واسمه صالح بن رستم » .

"Narrated Abū Dharr (رضى) about the Prophet (ﷺ) that he said: Don't show the slightest contempt for the concept of kindness. And if you don't find any good (deed) to do, meet your brother with a bright face." (Muslim and At-Tirmidhī)[10]

Ibn Kathīr concludes that Allah commands His creatures that they speak good speech to the people after He has commanded them with goodness to others in deed; thus, He unites between the extremities of goodness of deed and that of goodness of speech.

In their discussion of the second Qur'ānic injunction about parents of a general nature:

"And do good (show kindness) unto parents, and unto kinsfolk and orphans, and the needy." (4:36)

the three commentators express a re-statement of their previous opinions on the subject. Al-Qurṭubī however, includes an additional Ḥadīth, which succinctly expresses the importance of the child-parent relationship.

« روى شُعبة وهشيم الواسطيان عن يَعْلَى بن عطاء عن أبيه عن عبد ٱللّٰه بن عمرو بن العاص قال قال رسول ٱللّٰه ﷺ : رِضا الرّبّ فى رِضا الوالدين وسُخْطُه فى سُخْط الوالدين » .

"According to Shu'bah and Hashīm Al-Wāsṭiyān, 'Abdullah Ibn 'Amr Ibn Al-'Aṣ narrated that the Messenger of Allah (ﷺ) said: The satisfaction of the Lord is (in) the satisfaction of the parents, and the displeasure of the Lord is (in) the displeasure of the parents."[11]

The following Ḥadīths are a further illustration of the immense importance, in Islam, given to kindness and service to parents, in general, and to the mother, in particular.

« احفظ وُدَّ أبيك ، لا تقطعه فيُطفىءَ ٱللّٰه نورك » (البخارى فى الأدب - الطبرانى فى الأوسط ، البيهقى فى شعب الإيمان - عن ابن عباس) .

"Narrated Ibn 'Abbās: Safeguard the love for your parent. Do not cut it off or your light will be extinguished by Allah." (Al-Bukhārī in *Al-Adab;* Aṭ-Ṭabarānī in *Al-Awsaṭ;* Al-Baihaqī in *Shu'b Al-'Īmān*)[12]

« حدثنا أبو بكر بنُ أبى شَيْبَةَ حدثنا علىُّ بنُ مُسهِرٍ عن الشَّيْبانىّ عن الوليد بن العَيْزار عن سَعْد بنِ إياسٍ أبى عَمْرو الشَّيْبانىّ عن عَبْدِ آلله بن مسْعودٍ قال سألْتُ رسول آلله ﷺ أىُّ العملِ أفضلُ قال : الصّلاةُ لوقتها قال : قُلْتُ ثمّ أىٌّ قال : بِرّ الوالِدين قال : قُلْتُ ثمّ أىٌّ قال : الجهادُ فى سَبيلِ آلله » .

"Narrated 'Abdullah Ibn Mas'ūd: I asked the Messenger of Allah (ﷺ) which deed was the preferred one? He said: Prayer at its proper time. Then I asked: Which is next? He said: Kindness to parents. Then I asked: Which is next? He said: Fighting for the sake of Allah." (Muslim)[13]

« عن عبد آلله بن عمرو بن العاص قال : استأذن رجل رسول آلله ﷺ فى الجهاد ، فقال : أحىٌّ والداك ؟ قال نعم ، قال : فيهما فجاهد » .

"Narrated 'Abdullah Ibn 'Amr Ibn Al-'Āṣ (رضى): The Messenger of Allah (ﷺ) excused a man from *jihād.* He said: Are your parents alive? He said: Yes. He said: Then, (struggling) in their service is your *jihād.*" (Al-Bukhārī, Muslim, Abū Dāwūd, An-Nasā'ī and At-Tirmidhī)[14]

« عن أنس قال : أتى رجل إلى رسول آلله ﷺ فقال إنى أشتهى الجهاد ولا أقدر عليه ، قال : هل بقى من والديك أحد ؟ قال : أمّى قال : فآيل آلله فى برها فإذا فعلت ذلك فأنت حاج ومعتمر ومجاهد » .

"Narrated Anas (رضى): A man came to the Messenger of Allah (ﷺ) and said: I longed to go on *jihād* but I was not able to. He said: Is either one of your parents still alive? The man said: My mother. He said: Allah has instructed us in devotion to her, so if you do thus, you are as one who has made the *ḥajj,* the *'umrah* and participated in *jihād.*" (Abū Ya'lā and Aṭ-Ṭabarānī)[15]

« عن ابن عمر رضى آلله عنهما قال : أتى رجل رسول آلله ﷺ فقال : إنى أصبت ذنباً عظيما فهل لى من توبة ؟ قال : هل لك من أم ؟ قال : لا ، قال : هل لك من خالة ؟ قال : نعم ، قال فبرها » .

"Narrated Ibn 'Umar (رضى): A man came to the Messenger of Allah (ﷺ) and said: I committed a great sin. Is there anything I can do to repent? He said: Do you have a mother? The man said: No. He said: Do you have a maternal aunt? The man said: Yes. He said: Then, be kind and devoted to her." (At-Tirmidhī)[16]

« لو أدركتُ والدىَّ أو أحدهما وقد افتتحت صلاة العشاء وقرأتُ الفاتحة فدعتنى أمّى : يا محمدُ ! لأجَبتها » (أبو الشيخ – عن طلق بن علىّ) .

"Narrated Ṭalaq Ibn 'Alī: If I became aware of my parents, or one of them, and I had begun the *'Ishā'* prayer and recited Sūrat *Al-Fātiḥah*; then, my mother called me: O Muḥammad! I would have answered her." (Abū Ash-Shaikh)[17]

« لا تبرح من أمّك حتى تأذن لك أو يتوفاها الموت لأنه أعظم لأجرك » . (الطبرانى فى الكبير – عن ابن عباس) .

"Narrated Ibn 'Abbās: Do not leave your mother unless she gives you permission or death takes her, because that is the greatest (deed) for your reward." (Aṭ-Ṭabarānī in *Al-Kabīr*)[18]

« من قَبَّلَ بين عينى أمِهِّ كان له ستراً من النار » (ابن عدى – البيهقى فى شعب الإيمان – عن ابن عباس) .

"Narrated Ibn 'Abbās: Whoever kissed his mother between the eyes had protection from the Fire." (Ibn 'Addī; Al-Baihaqī in *Shu'b Al-'Īmān*)[19]

With respect to financial responsibility for needy parents the Qur'ān addresses this point clearly:

> "That which ye spend for good (must go) to parents and near kindred and orphans and the needy and the wayfarer." (2:215)

Thus, amongst the category of needy persons to whom financial support is due, parents come first. The consensus of opinion of the three commentators is that this verse implies the appropriateness of voluntary charity to needy parents, above and beyond the annually required compulsory charity (*az-zakāt*).

Aṭ-Ṭabarī states that the reference is to voluntary charity. Ibn Kathīr concurs with Aṭ-Ṭabarī's discussion, but also presents Muqātil Ibn Ḥayyān's opinion that this was subsequently abrogated by *az-zakāt.* Al-Qurṭubī says it was not abrogated and that they are two different issues, one being voluntary charity and the other compulsory charity.

Aṭ-Ṭabarī's explication re-emphasizes the fact that the Qur'ānic injunction refers to both parents, the mother as well as the father. Thus, he says the meaning of the verse is: Your Companions, O Muḥammad, ask you what they should spend out of their wealth on voluntary charity, and on whom they should spend it. So, say to them: What you spend of your wealth as voluntary charity, use it for your fathers and your mothers and your relatives, and the orphans amongst you and the needy and the wayfarers. Thereby, that which you do of good, doing it for them, indeed Allah is aware of it, and He records for you, until you die, your reward for it on the Day of Ressurection. And He rewards you for what you gave of kindness. Thus, the « خير » that the Most Lofty, May He Be Praised, stated in this verse of His, is the wealth, the spending of which, the Companions asked the Messenger of Allah (ﷺ) about, and Allah answered them in this verse.[20] Al-Qurṭubī specifies the Companion for whom the verse was revealed as 'Amr Ibn Al-Jamūh, who was, at that time, an old man. He said: O Messenger of Allah, my wealth is great, so what should I give in charity, and on whom should I spend? Consequently, according to Al-Qurṭubī this verse was revealed.[21]

Ibn Kathīr records, in reference to Ibn Ḥayyān's comment above that As-Suddī said there is speculation about this; in other words, it is not a generally accepted opinion.[22] Al-Qurṭubī clarifies his position on the question posed by Ibn Ḥayyān's opinion, stating that Ibn Jurīj and others said: *Az-zakāt* is different from the spending mentioned in this verse; therefore, there is no abrogation of it. He goes on to say that it is clearly the spending of voluntary charity, and it is obligatory on the man of means that he spends on his needy parents what is suitable for their status and compatible with his (financial) status, for food and clothing, etc.[23]

This primacy of concern for parents' needs is expressly illustrated by the following excerpt from a longer Ḥadīth:

« حدثنى محَمدُ بن إسحٰقَ المُسَيَّبِىُّ حدثنى أَنسُ (يعى ابن عياض أبا ضَمْرة) عن مُوسى بن عُقْبة عن نافعٍ عن عبد آللّٰه بن عُمَرَ عن رسول آللّٰه ﷺ أنّهُ قال بينما ثلاثةُ نَفَرٍ يتمشَّوْنَ أَخذهم المطرُ فأوَوا إلى غارٍ فى جبلٍ فانحطّتْ على فم غارهم صخرةٌ من الجبلِ فانطبقتْ عليهم فقال بَعْضُهم لبعض أنظُروا أعمالًا عملتموها صالحةً لله فادعوا آللّٰه تعالى بها لعلّ يفرجُها عنكم فقال أحدُهم اللّهمَّ إنّهُ كان لى والدان شيخان كبيران وإمرأتى ولى صِبْية صِغارٌ أرْعَى عليهم فاذا أرحْتُ عليهم حلبْتُ فبدأتُ بوالدىَّ فسَقيْتُهما قبل بنىَّ وأنّهُ نأى بى ذات يوم الشّجرُ فلم آت حتّى أمْسَيْتُ فوجدْتُهما قد ناما فحلبْتُ كما كنْتُ أحْلُبُ فجئْتُ بالحلابِ فقمتُ عند رُؤُسِهما أكرهُ أن أوقظهما من نَوْمهما وأكرهُ أن أَسْقَى الصِّبْيه قبلهما والصِّبْية يتضاغَوْنَ عند قدمَىَّ فلمْ يزلْ ذٰلك دأْبِي ودأبهم حتى طَلَعَ الفجْرُ فإنْ كنْتَ تَعْلمُ أنّى فعلْتُ ذٰلك ابتغاء وجهِكَ فافْرُجْ لنا منها فُرْجَةً نرى منها السّماء ففَرَجَ آللّٰه منها فُرْجةً » .

"'Abdullah Ibn 'Umar reported that Allah's Messenger (ﷺ) said: Three persons set out on a journey. They were overtaken by rain and they had to find protection in a mountain cave, when at its mouth there fell a rock of that mountain, and thus blocked them altogether. One of them said to the others: Look at your good deeds that you performed for the sake of Allah and then supplicate Allah the Exalted, that He might rescue you (from this trouble). One of them said: O Allah, I had my parents who were old

> and my wife and my small children also. I tended the flock and when I came back to them in the evening, I did the milking and served that milk to my parents, before serving my children. One day when I was obliged to go out to a distant place in search of fodder and could not come back before evening and found them (the parents) asleep, I milked the animals as usual and brought milk to them and stood at their heads avoiding disturbing them from sleep and I did not deem it advisable to serve milk to my children before serving them. I remained there in that state and my parents too until morning. And (O Allah) if Thou art aware that I did this in order to seek Thy pleasure, give us an opening that we may see the sky. And Allah gave them an opening." (Muslim)[24]

Sūrah 6, Verse 151 re-emphasizes the parallel between submission to Allah, the One, and submission to His command to good treatment of parents:

> "... that ye ascribe nothing as partner unto Him, and that ye do good to parents ..." (6:151)

However, the commentary on this verse further reveals that this obligation is due regardless of similarity or difference of religion, i.e., the Muslim is bound to offer respect and service to parents, whether they be Muslims, Christians, Jews or even polytheists.

Al-Qurṭubī says that grammatically, the word « الإحسان » is a noun *maṣdar* in the accusative case, which is made accusative by a missing verb; thus the implied meaning is: Do the highest degree of good to your parents. He further defines « الإحسان » to parents as: respecting them, protecting them, caring for them, obedience to their command, while not treating them as slaves, but rather giving them the position of authority.[25] Ibn Kathīr points out that the comparison between submission to Allah and reverence to parents is mentioned many times in the Qur'ān, and adds that if the parents are non-believers, showing kindness and respect to them is sufficient;[26] thus implying that the Muslim is bound to his obligations to his parents, with the exception of parental commands which are contra-Islam.

The two following Ḥadīths illustrate the insistence in Islam on reverence and kindness to one's mother, regardless of religious difference.

« عن شقيق بن وائل قال : ماتت أمّي نصرانيةً فأتيت عمر بن الخطاب فذكرتُ ذلك له فقال : اركب دابةً وسِره أمام جنازتها » (المحاملي ، ابن عسَاكر) .

"Narrated Shaqīq Ibn Wā'il: My mother died a Christian, so I went to 'Umar Ibn Al-Khaṭṭāb and told him that. And he said: Mount an animal and ride in front of her bier (in front of the funeral procession)." (Al-Muḥāmalī; Ibn 'Asākir)[27]

« حدثنا أبو كُرَيْب محّمدُ بن العَلَاء حدثنا أبو أسامة عنِ هِشام عن أبيه عن أسماء بنت أبي بكر قالتْ قَدَمَتْ عليَّ أمّي وهي مُشْركةٌ في عهد قريش إذ عاهَدَهم فاستفْتَيْتُ رسول آلله ﷺ فقُلْتُ يارسول آلله قدمتْ عليَّ أمّي وهي راغبة أفأصِلُ أمّي قال : نعم صِلِي أمّك » .

"Asmā' bint Abū Bakr (رضى) reported: My mother who was a polytheist came to me when he (the Prophet (ﷺ) entered into treaty with the Quraish (of Makkah). I inquired from the Messenger of Allah (ﷺ) saying: O Messenger of Allah, my mother has come to me and she is inclined (or afraid); should I show her kindness? He said: Yes, treat her kindly." (Muslim)[28]

When parents reach the period of old age, this is the time which offers the Muslim the greatest opportunity to fulfil his obligations to them, and thus hope to gain Allah's pleasure. Muslims are counselled to keep in mind the fact that their elderly parents were devoted to them when they were in need of care as a child, while at the same time, to remember that they are parents, not children, with all the rights and privileges due to them as such.

The Qur'ān speaks directly to the question of treatment of parents in old age:

"Thy Lord hath decreed, that ye worship none save Him, and (that ye show) kindness to parents. If one of them or both of them attain old age with thee, say not 'Uff' to them nor repulse them, but speak to them graciously. And lower unto them the wing of submission through mercy, and say: My Lord! Have mercy on them both as they did care for me when I was little." (17:23-24)

and stresses the obligation to them and the nature of it in the following verse:

"And dutiful toward his parents, and he was not arrogant, rebellious." (19:14)

In discussion of Sūrah 17, Verses 23-24, Aṭ-Ṭabarī and Ibn Kathīr apply their previous comments on the child-parent relationship with some specification for the period of old age. Al-Qurṭubī, however, uses these verses as an opportunity to give his full exegesis on the subject.

Aṭ-Ṭabarī emphasizes that due to the words « وَقَضَى رَبُّكَ » this is a command from Allah to show kindness to parents, to do good to them and to respect them. He says the meaning is not to grumble (mutter a complaint) about something that you see in one of them, or both, a kind of muttering that people are hurt by, but rather, to be patient with them in anticipation of (spiritual) reward, as they were patient with you when you were young.[29] He then refers to Mujāhid's statement that the reference, in these verses, is to the case where your parents are senile, in the condition of faeces and urine, as you were as a baby, and you say "Uff" to them.[30] As further comment on the meaning of "Uff", Aṭ-Ṭabarī includes 'Atā' Ibn Abī Rabāḥ's statement, on the authority of Muḥammad Ibn Ismā'īl Al-Aḥmasī: Don't brush your parents aside, i.e., don't treat them as if they were insignificant. Having stated what not to do, the verse describes what to do by stating « وَقُلْ لَهُما قَوْلًا كَرِيمًا », explained by Ibn Jurīj, on the authority of Al-Qāsim as: The best that you can find of speech.[31]

Al-Qurṭubī says that reverence and goodness to parents is that you do not insult or blaspheme them because this is, without argument, one of the major sins. To qualify his statement, and to illustrate the depth of its meaning, Al-Qurṭubī refers to the following Ḥadīth:

« فى صحيح مسلم عن عبد آلله بن عمرو أن رسول آلله ﷺ قال : إن مِنْ الكبائر شَتْمُ الرجل والديه . قالوا : يارسول آلله ، وهل يشْتمُ الرجل والديه ؟ قال : نعم ، يسُبّ الرجل أبا الرجل فيسُبّ أباه ويسُبُّ أمَّهُ فيسُبُّ أمّه » .

"'Abdullah Ibn 'Amr narrated that the Messenger of Allah (ﷺ) said: Indeed abuse of a man's parents is one of the major sins. They said: O Messenger of Allah, does a man abuse his parents? He said: Yes. The man insults the father of (another) man, so the (other) man insults the first one's father, and he insults the other one's mother and vice-versa." (*Ṣaḥīḥ Muslim*)[32]

Also, in another Ḥadīth the blasphemer of parents is placed on a par with the idol-worshipper and the innovator:

« لعن آلله من لعن والديه ! ولعن آلله من ذبح لغير آلله ! ولعن آلله من آوى مُحْدِثاً ! ولعن آلله من غيَّر منار الأرض » (أحمد ، مسلم ، النسائى – عن علىّ) .

"Narrated 'Alī: Allah cursed whoever cursed his parents! And Allah cursed whoever sacrificed to other than Allah! And Allah cursed whoever accomodated an innovator! And Allah cursed whoever changed the boundary lines of the land!" (Aḥmad; Muslim; An-Nasā'ī)[33]

In his commentary on this Ḥadīth, An-Nawawī confirms that the cursing of the father and mother is one of the major sins. To explain the rest of the Ḥadīth, An-Nawawī says that the indication of « منار الأرض » is the limits (boundaries) of it. And as for sacrificing to other than Allah, the indication by it is that one sacrifices in the name of other than Allah, the Most High, like he who sacrifices to the idols or to the cross or to Mūsā (ﷺ) or to 'Īsā (ﷺ) or to the Ka'bah, etc.[34]

Al-Qurṭubī says that the condition of old age is specified in verse 23 because this is the state in which parents need kindness because of the change in their condition to weakness and old age. With regard to their condition, more kindness and compassion is required, because in this state they have become more troublesome. In addition, since the burden is the man's duty and is something he has to live with daily, irritation develops and vexation increases; then his anger towards his parents appears, and he flies into a rage at them and becomes arrogant with the boldness of his position and the lack of religion. Al-Qurṭubī says the despicable is what he exhibits by indicating his irritation by repeated "heavy breaths". Instead, he was commanded by Allah to receive them with speech characterized by respect, the doing of which is the security against shameful acts. Al-Qurṭubī includes Abū Rajā Al-'Aṭāriḍī's statement that "Uff" is speech which is maligning, mean and concealed. In reference to Mujāhid's above-mentioned statement included by Aṭ-Ṭabarī, Al-Qurṭubī says that the verse is more general than that and that it refers to the saying of "Uff" to everything that vexes or is a burden.[35]

« روى من حديث علىّ بن أبى طالب رضى آلله عنهُ قال قال رسول آلله ﷺ : لو علم آلله من عقوق شيئا أردأ مِنْ « أف » لذكره فليعمل البارّ ماشاء أن يعمل فلن يدخل النار ، وليعمل العاق ماشاء أن يعمل فلن يدخل الجنة » .

> "It is related from a Ḥadīth of 'Alī Ibn Abī Ṭālib (رضى) that he said that the Messenger of Allah (ﷺ) said: If Allah knew any type of rudeness worse than "Uff", He would have mentioned it, so do of the righteous acts what you want to do and you will not enter the Fire, and do of the disrespectful acts what you want to do and you will not enter Paradise."[36]

As commentary on this Ḥadīth, the *'Ulamā'* said: Accordingly, one's saying "Uff" to parents becomes the worst thing, because the rejection of them is an ungrateful rejection and a repudiation of one's up-bringing, and a rejection of the counsel given in the Qur'ān. To prove his point that "Uff" is not an expression to be taken lightly, Al-Qurṭubī gives the example of the Prophet Ibrāhīm's (ﷺ) use of it to show his rejection of idols and idol worshippers, in which Ibrāhīm (ﷺ) said to his people: "Uff" to you and all that you worship instead of Allah." (21:67). In addition, Al-Qurṭubī states that the meaning of « النهر » is rebuke and harshness.[37]

To explain the meaning of « وَقُل لَهُما قَوْلاً كَرِيما » Al-Qurṭubī refers to 'Aṭā's statement in which he says it is polite gentleness; for example, saying: "O my father and O my mother", without calling them directly by either their first names or their last names.[38] In reference to this part of the verse, Abū Al-Baddāh (Al-Haddāj) At-Tujībī said, "I said to Sa'īd Ibn Al-Musayyib: Everything that is in the Qur'ān about reverence to parents, I have understood except His statement: 'And speak to them graciously'." Ibn Al-Musayyib said, "This refers to the sinner slave's speaking rude harsh words to the master." Al-Qurṭubī goes on to say that the lending of affection and mercy to parents and submission to them is the submission of the governed to the leader, and that of the slave to the master as Sa'īd Ibn Al-Musayyib indicated. Thus, the intention of the ruling of this verse is that the person should put himself in a state of maximum submission with respect to his parents, in his speech and his silence and his looks, and should not give them sharp looks, as this is the look of the angered.[39]

In Aṭ-Ṭabarī's explication of verse 24, he quotes a statement on the authority of Al-Qāsim, on the authority of Hishām Ibn 'Urwah from his father, that 'Umar Ibn Al-Khaṭṭāb(رضى) said: Don't refuse to do anything they want.[40] Al-Qurṭubī clarifies this point by stating that rudeness to parents is the contradiction of their desires which are legally permissible, just as respecting them is the acceptance of their desires which are legally permissible. Thus, if both or one of them commands, obedience to them is a must if that command is not a sin and if that which is commanded is « مباح »(of the permissible type); likewise, if it is « مندوب »(of the recommended type). Further, some people hold the view that the parents' command, which is "permissible" becomes a "recommended" right of the child, and their command which is "recommended" is increased to be even more highly recommended.[41]

Al-Qurṭubī mentions Abū Hurairah's Ḥadīth that kindness and compassion to the mother should be three times that to the father,[42] and relates it to his discussion of obedience. He mentions similar points to those made by An-Nawawī, and adds that if you come to this conclusion, then the meaning is judged to be an obligation on the individual or « شهد له العيان ».[43] Then, he presents various opinions about this point and his own conclusion. First is a contrary opinion. It is reported about Mālik that a man said to him: My father is in the country of the Sudan and he wrote to me that I should come to him, but my mother prevents me from doing so. Then, he (Mālik) said to him: Obey your father and disobey your mother. Thus, Mālik's statement indicates that reverence to both parents is equal as far as he is concerned. Then, Al-Laith was asked about this question, and he commanded (the asker) with obedience to the mother, claiming that she gets two-thirds of the devotion. Al-Qurṭubī concludes, however, that Abū Hurairah's Ḥadīth indicates that she gets three-fourths of the devotion, and that it is proof to those who dispute the matter. Al-Muḥāsibī affirms in his book *Kitāb Ar-Ra'āyah* that there is no disagreement amongst the *'Ulamā'* that the mother gets three-fourths of the devotion and the father one-fourth according to Abū Hurairah's (رضى) Ḥadīth. (And Allah knows best).[44]

In his discussion of « من الرحمة » Al-Qurṭubī says that « من » indicates "the kind of", i.e., that the "lowering of the wing" be of a merciful submitting of the spirit, not that it be in actions only. So the Most High ordered His slaves to be merciful to their parents and to pray for them. Thus, you should be compassionate to them as they were to you, and befriend them as they did you, remembering that when you were an incapable, needy child, they preferred you to themselves, and they stayed awake nights, and went hungry while they satisfied your appetite, and were in need of clothes while they clothed you. So, reward them when they reach old age in the condition that you were in as a child, in that you treat them as they did you, and give kindness to them priority.[45]

« قال ابن عباس قال النبى ﷺ : من أمسى مُرْضياً لوالديه وأصبح أمسى وأصبح وله بابان مفتوحان من الجنة وإن واحدا فواحدا ، ومن أمسى وأصبح مُسْخطا لوالديه أمسى وأصبح وله بابان مفتوحان إلى النار وإن واحدا فواحدا ، فقال : يارسول الله ، وإن ظلماه؟ قال : وإن ظلماه وإن ظلماه وإن ظلماه » .

"Ibn 'Abbās said that the Prophet (ﷺ) said: He who ends the day and his parents are satisfied with him and begins the day thus, ends and begins the day, and to him, two doors to Paradise are opened; and if it is one parent, then one door. And he who ends and begins the day and is the object of odiousness to his parents, he ends and begins the day and to him, two doors to the Fire are opened, and if it is one parent, then one door. Then, a man said: O Messenger of Allah, and if they have mistreated (oppressed) him? He said: And (even) if they have mistreated him, and even if they have mistreated him and even if they have mistreated him."[46]

In the commentary on Sūrah 19, Verse 14, the emphasis is on the importance of obedience to parents, by way of example of the Prophet Yaḥyā (ﷺ) who is praised for his consistent submissiveness and humbleness to Allah and to his parents, doing what he was commanded to do and refraining from what he was forbidden.[47] The following Ḥadīths are further illustrations of the requirement in Islam for such respect and submissiveness to one's mother and father, and an indication of what constitutes disobedience:

« قال الإمام أحمد حدثنا خلف بن الوليد حدثنا ابن عياش عن يحيى بن سعد عن
خالد بن معدان عن المقدام بن معد يكرب عن النبى ﷺ قال : إن آلله يوصيكم
بآبائكم إن آلله يوصيكم بأمهاتكم إن آلله يوصيكم بأمهاتكم إن آلله يوصيكم
بأمهاتكم إن آلله يوصيكم بالأقرب فالأقرب » .

"Narrated Al-Miqdām Ibn Ma'dīkarib that the Prophet (ﷺ) said: Indeed Allah has warned you about (your responsibility to) your fathers, indeed, Allah has warned you about (your responsibility to) your mothers; indeed Allah has warned you about (your responsibility to) your mothers; indeed Allah has warned you about (your responsibility to) your mothers; indeed Allah has warned you about (your responsibility to) your relatives; so your relatives." (Al-Imām Aḥmad)[48]

« قال الإمام أحمد حدثنا حجاج ومحمد بن جعفر قال حدثنا شعبة عن قتادة سمعت ، زرارة بن أوفى يحدث عن أبى مالك القشيرى قال : قال النبى ﷺ : من أدرك والديه أو أحدهما ثم دخل النار من بعد ذلك فأبعده آلله وسحقه» .

"Narrated Abū Mālik Al-Qushairī, the Prophet (ﷺ) said: Whoever's parents, or one of them, died and then he entered the Fire, Allah will disassociate Himself from him and destroy him." (Al-Imām Aḥmad).[49] (In other words, being kind to his parents, etc. would have saved him from the Fire, so obviously he did not do so.)

« حدّثنا زُهيْرُ بنُ حَرْب حدثنا جَرِيرٌ عن سُهَيلٍ عن أبيه عن أبى هُرَيْرَةَ قال رسولُ آللهِ ﷺ رَغِمَ أَنْفُهُ ثمَّ رغمَ أَنْفُهُ ثمّ رَغمَ أَنْفُهُ قيل مَنْ يارسول آلله قال مَنْ أدْرَكَ والِدَيْهِ عِنْدَ الكِبَرِ أحَدَهُما أوْكِلَيْهِما ثمّ لم يَدْخُلِ الجَنَّة» .

"Abū Hurairah (رضى) reported Allah's Messenger (ﷺ) as saying: Let him be humbled (let his pride be in the dust); let him be humbled; let him be humbled. It was said: O Messenger of Allah, who is he? He said: He who finds his parents in old age, either one of them or both of them, and does not enter Paradise." (Muslim)[50]

An-Nawawī comments, "Let his pride be in the dust" for not revering his parents with his service to them or providing for them, thus, he lost his chance for Paradise.[51]

« عن عبد آلله بن عمرو قال : جاء رجل إلى النبى ﷺ يبايعه على الهجرة ترك أبويه يبكيان فقال : ارجع إليهما فأضحكهما كما أبكيتهما » .

"Narrated 'Abdullah Ibn 'Amr: A man came to the Prophet (ﷺ) pledging himself to go on the *hijrah.* He left his parents crying. So, he (the Prophet (ﷺ)) said: Return to them and make them laugh as you have made them cry." (Abū Dāwūd; An-Nasā'ī; Aḥmad; Ibn Mājah; Al-Ḥākim)[52]

« من أحزن والديه فقد عقهما » (الخطيب فى الجامع – عن علىّ) .

"Narrated 'Alī (رضى): Whoever saddens his parents, has disobeyed them." (Al-Khaṭīb in *Al-Jāmi'*)[53]

« عن عبد آلله بن عمرو بن العاص رضى آلله عنهما عن النبى ﷺ أنه قال : الكبائِرُ الإِشْراكُ بالله ، وعُقوقُ الوالِدَيْنِ ، وقَتْلُ النّفسِ ، واليمينُ الغموسُ » .

"Narrated 'Abdullah Ibn 'Amr Ibn Al-'Āṣ (رضى) about the Prophet (ﷺ) that he said: The major sins are associating anything with Allah, and rudeness to parents, and killing anyone and swearing a false oath purposefully." (Al-Bukhārī)[54]

« عن أبى عيسَى المغيرة بن شعبة رضى آلله عنه عن النبى ﷺ : إنَّ آلله حَرَّمَ عليكم عقوق الأمهات » .

From a longer Ḥadīth: "Narrated Abū 'Īsā Al-Mughīrah (رضى) that the Prophet (ﷺ) said: Verily, Allah forbade for you, rudeness (disobedience) to mothers." (Al-Bukhārī and Muslim)[55]

Respect and kindness to the mother extends even beyond the point of death. This includes prayer for her forgiveness, and the completion of various obligations to her. The Qur'ān provides examples of such prayers for believing parents and a reminder to the Muslim to be grateful for having this opportunity:

"Our Lord! Forgive me and my parents and the believers on the Day of Reckoning." (14:41)

"My Lord! Arouse me to be thankful for Thy favour wherewith Thou hast favoured me and my parents." (27:19)

"My Lord! Forgive me and my parents and him who entereth my house believing, and believing men and believing women." (71:28)

The three commentators apparently find the meaning of these verses obvious, such that they do not require additional explication. However, in Al-Qurṭubī's previous discussion of "as they did care for me" in Sūrah 17, Verse 24, he mentions that the reference is to believing parents, as the Qur'ān abrogated asking for forgiveness for the non-believers even if they were the closest relatives:

> "It is not for the Prophet and those who believe to pray for the forgiveness of idolators even though they may be near of kin." (9:113)

Thus, if the Muslim's parents are non-believers, he should treat them as Allah has commanded him to, with respect, kindness, etc., except for the mercy to them after death as non-believers because this alone was invalidated by the verse mentioned. An additional comment clarifies that prayer for mercy in this world for the nonbelieving parents as long as they live is not invalidated by this verse.[56]

The following Ḥadīth is an illustration of this verse, and the commentary confirms Al-Qurṭubī's conclusion:

« حَدثنا يَحيَى بْنُ أيُّوب ومُحَمَّدُ بْنُ عَبّاد واللفظُ ليحْيى قالا حَدثنا مَرْوانُ بْنُ مُعاوِيَةَ عن يزيدَ يعنى ابن كَيْسَانَ عن أبى حازم عن أبى هُريرةَ قال قال رسول الله ﷺ استأذَنْتُ ربّى أنْ أسْتَغْفِرَ لأمّى فَلَمْ يأْذنْ لى واستأذَنْتُ أن أَزورَ قبْرَها فَأَذَنَ لِي » .

> "Narrated Abū Hurairah that the Messenger of Allah (ﷺ) said: I asked my Lord's permission to ask forgiveness for my mother, and He did not allow me to do so. And I asked for His permission to visit her grave, and He allowed me to do so." (Muslim)[57]

An-Nawawī's commentary on this Ḥadīth is that contained in it is the allowance for visiting the polytheist during lifetime and the grave after death. His argument is that if permission is given to visit the polytheist after death, then, it must include during the lifetime, because this has more priority and is in accordance with Allah's command of the best of companionship to all parents during one's lifetime. He goes on to say that contained in this Ḥadīth is the prohibition of asking forgiveness for non-believers (after death).[58]

The following Ḥadīth indicates that a reward is forthcoming for the one who visits his parents' grave:

« من زار قبر والديه أو أحدهما فى كل جمعةٍ مرةً غفر ٱللّٰه له وكُتِبَ بَراً» (الحكيم عن أبى هريرة) .

"Narrated Abū Hurairah: Whoever visits his parents' grave or one of them, once every week, Allah forgives him, and he would be recorded as righteous." (Al-Ḥakīm)[59]

The next two Ḥadīths indicate additional obligations due to parents after death and the reward for fulfilling them:

« حدثنا ابراهيم بن مهدى وعثمان أبى شيبة ومحمد بن علاء المعنى قال حدثنا عبد ٱللّٰه بن ادريس عن عبد الرحمن بن سليمان عن أسيد بن على بن عبيد مولى بنى ساعدة عن أبيه عن أبى أسيد مالك بن ربيعة السّاعدى قال بينا نحن عند رسول ٱللّٰه ﷺ إذ جاء رجل من بنى سلمة فقال : يارسول ٱللّٰه هل بقى من بر أبوى شىء أبرّهما بعد موتهما ؟ قال نعم ، الصلاة عليهما والاستغفار لهما وانفاذ عهدهما من بعدهما وصلة الرحم التى لا توصل إلا بهما ، وإكرام صديقهما » (أخرجه أبو داود).

"Narrated Abū Asīd Mālik Ibn Rabī'ah As-Sā'adī while we were with the Messenger of Allah (ﷺ) when a man from Banī Sallamah came and he said: O Messenger of Allah (ﷺ) is there any remaining chance to show devotion to my parents after they have died? He said: Yes, prayer for them and asking forgiveness for them and the fulfilment of their contracts after them and the keeping up of family relations that they used to maintain and the respecting of their friends." (Abū Dāwūd)[60]

« من حجَّ عن والديه أو قضى عنهما مَغْرَماً بعثه ٱللّٰه يوم القيامة مع الأبرار » (الطبرانى فى الأوسط ، الدارقطنى – عن ابن عباس) . مغرماً : دَيْناً .

"Narrated Ibn 'Abbās: Whoever performs the pilgrimage for his parents or terminates a debt for them, Allah sends him forth with the righteous on the Day of Ascension." (Ad-Dārqaṭanī; Aṭ-Ṭabarānī in *Al-Awsaṭ*)[61]

In summary, according to Islam, gratitude to parents is on the highest human level, such that it is compared with the ultimate gratitude, that due to Allah. Service to parents is second only to prayer and its fulfilment to elderly parents absolves one from participation in *jihād*. Good treatment of parents, in their lifetime and after death, is an established right due to them, not a gratuitous act, and involves all aspects of human behaviour, great or small, to be expressed to the limits of human feasibility. Furthermore, utmost respect is due them, regardless of religion, physical condition or social status. The concern and respect for the mother, specifically, is an expiator of sin and a clear way for the believer to become closer to Allah and to ward off the Fire.

NOTES

[1]Khān, Bāb Mā Warada Fī Birr Al-Wālidah, p. 236.

[2]'Alā' Ad-Dīn 'Alī Al-Muttaqā Ibn Ḥusām Ad-Dīn Al-Hindī, *Kanz Al-'Umāl Fī Sunan Al-Aqwāl* (Hyderabad: Dā'irah Al-Ma'ārif Al-'Uthmāniyyah, 1364 Heg.), v. 16, p. 463 (No. 45453).

[3]*Ṣaḥīḥ Al-Bukhārī* (Chicago, Ill.: Kazi Pub., 1979), v. 8, Kitāb Al-Adab, Chap. 1, No. 2, p. 2; Khān, Bāb Mā Warada Fī Birr Al-Wālidah, p. 235. Also, see: Ismail 'Abdul Razack and 'Abdul Jawad Al-Banna, *Women and Family in the Sunnah of the Prophet* (Al-Azhar: Dār Al-Kutub), p. 32 for Ibn Māni's narration of this Ḥadīth.

[4]Abū Al-Ḥasan Muslim Ibn Al Ḥajjāj, *Ṣaḥīḥ Muslim: Bi Sharḥ An-Nawawī* (Egypt, 1924), v. 16, Kitāb Al-Birr Wa Aṣ-Ṣilah Wa Al-Adab, p. 102.

[5]Abū Ja'far Muḥammad Jarīr Aṭ-Ṭabarī, *Jāmi' Al-Bayān 'An Ta'wil Āiy Al-Qur'ān* (Cairo: Muṣṭafā Al-Ḥalabī, 3rd printing, 1968), v. 1. p. 390.

[6]Al-Imām 'Imād Ad-Dīn Abī Al-Fidā' Ismā'īl Ibn Kathīr Al-Qurashī Ad-Dimashqī, *Tafsīr Al-Qur'ān Al-'Aẓīm* (Egypt: Dār Iḥyā' Al-Kutub Al-'Arabiyyah) v. 1, p. 119.

[7]Abū 'Abdullah Muḥammad Ibn Aḥmad Al-Anṣārī Al-Qurṭubī, *Al-Jāmi' Li Aḥkām Al-Qur'ān* (Egypt: Dār Al-Kutub, 1967), v. 2, p. 13.

[8]Aṭ-Ṭabarī, v. 1. p. 390; Al-Qurṭubī, v. 2, p. 13.

[9]Ibn Kathīr, v. 1, p. 120.

[10]Ibid.

[11]Al-Qurṭubī, v. 5, p. 183.

[12]*Kanz,* v. 16, p. 464 (No. 45460).

[13]*Ṣaḥīḥ Muslim,* v. 2, Kitāb Al-'Īmān, Bāb Afḍal Al-A'māl, p. 73.

[14]Khān, Bāb Mā Warada Fī Birr Al-Wālidah, p. 236.

[15]Ibid., Bāb Mā Warada Fī Birr Al-Wālidain, p. 514.

[16]Ibid., Bāb Mā Warada Fī Birr Al-Wālidah, p. 237.

[17]*Kanz,* v. 16, p. 470 (No. 45500). (See below, Part I, Chap. III, p. 40 for Al-Qurṭubī's clarification of this point).

[18]Ibid., p. 472 (No. 45504).

[19]Ibid., p. 462 (No. 45442).

[20]Aṭ-Ṭabarī, v. 2, p. 342.

[21]Al-Qurṭubī, v. 3, p. 36.

[22]Ibn Kathīr, v. 1, p. 251.

[23]Al-Qurṭubī, v. 3, p. 37.

[24]*Ṣaḥīḥ Muslim,* v. 17, Kitāb Ar-Riqāq, p. 55-56.

[25]Al-Qurṭubī, v. 7, p. 132.

[26]Ibn Kathīr, v. 2, pp. 187-188.

[27]*Kanz,* v. 16, p. 577 (No. 45929).

[28]*Ṣaḥīḥ Muslim,* v. 7, Kitāb Az-Zakāt, Bāb Faḍl An-Nafaqah Wa Aṣ-Ṣadaqah 'Alā Al-Aqrabīn Wa Az-Zauj Wa Al-Awlād, p. 89.

[29]Aṭ-Ṭabarī, v. 15, p. 63.

[30]Ibid., v. 15, p. 64.

[31]Ibid., v. 15, p. 65.

[32]Al-Qurṭubī, v. 10, p. 238. Also, Abū Zakarīyā Yaḥyā Ibn Sharaf An-Nawawī, *Riyāḍ Aṣ-Ṣāliḥīn,* (Beirut: Dār Al-Fikr), Bāb Taḥrīm Al-'Uqūq Wa Qaṭī'ah Ar-Raḥm, p. 108 (No. 338).

[33]*Kanz,* v. 16, p. 480 (No. 45546).

[34]*Ṣaḥīḥ Muslim Bi Sharḥ An-Nawawī,* Kitāb Al-Aḍāḥī, Bāb Taḥrīm Adh-Dhabḥ Li Ghair Allah Ta'ālā Wa La'n Fā'ilihi, v. 13, p. 141.

[35]Al-Qurṭubī, v. 10, pp. 241-242.

[36]Ibid., v. 10, p. 243.

[37]Ibid.

[38]Ibid., Also, see Khān, Bāb Mā Nazala Fī 'iẓam Ḥaqq Al-Wālidain Wa Al-Iḥsān Ilaihimā Wa Ila Al-Mamlūkāt, p. 80 and Bāb Mā Nazala Fī Al-Iḥsan Ila Al-Wālidain Wa Nahā Al-Walad 'An Zajar Al-Wālid, pp. 114-115.

[39]Ibid., v. 10, pp. 243-244.

[40]Aṭ-Ṭabarī, v. 15, p. 65.

[41]Al-Qurṭubī, v. 10, p. 238.

[42]See p. 8 for the full text and An-Nawawī's commentary.

[43]Al-Qurṭubī, v. 10, p. 239.

[44]Ibid.

[45]Ibid., v. 10, p. 244.

[46]Ibid., v. 10, p. 245.

[47]Aṭ-Ṭabarī, v. 12, p. 58.

[48]Ibn Kathīr, v. 3, p. 35.

[49]Ibid.

[50]*Ṣaḥīḥ Muslim,* v. 16, Kitāb Al-Birr Wa Aṣ-Ṣilah Wa Al-Adab, Bāb Taqdīm Al-Wālidain 'Alā At-Taṭawwu' Bi Aṣ-Ṣalāt Wa Ghairihā, p. 109.

[51]Ibid., *Sharḥ An-Nawawī,* v. 16, pp. 108-109.

[52]*Kanz,* v. 16, p. 477 (No. 45532). Also, Khān, Bāb Mā Warada Fī Birr Al-Wālidah, p. 236.

[53]*Kanz,* v. 16, p. 478 (No. 45537).

[54]*Riyāḍ Aṣ-Ṣāliḥīn,* Bāb Taḥrīm Al-'Uqūq Wa Qaṭī'ah Ar-Raḥm, p. 107 (No. 337).

[55]Ibid., p. 108 (No. 340).

[56]Al-Qurṭubī, v. 10, pp. 244-245.

[57]*Ṣaḥīḥ Muslim,* v. 7, Kitāb Al-Janā'iz, Bāb Isti'dhān An-Nabī(ﷺ)Rabbahu Fī Ziyārat Qabr Ummihi, p. 45.

[58]Ibid., *Sharḥ An-Nawawī.*

[59]*Kanz,* v. 16, p. 468 (No. 45487).

[60]Abū Dāwūd Sulaymān Ibn Al-Ash'ath As-Sijistānī, *As-Sunan* (Egypt: Maktabah Al-'Arab, 1863) v. 2, Kitāb Al-Adab Bāb Fī Birr Al-Wālidain, pp. 216-217.

[61]*Kanz*, v. 16, p. 468 (No. 45485).

CHAPTER II

INHERITANCE

The laws of inheritance are for the most part specified clearly in the Qur'ān; consequently, the discussion rests with the application of the law, and those areas which go beyond the text, while having bearing on the mother. Within the context of illustrating the application of the law, points which need clarification are the status of the non-Muslim mother and that of the grandmother.

The first verse revealed on the subject of inheritance involved the making of a will:

> "It is prescribed for you, when death approacheth one of you, if he leave wealth, that he bequeath unto parents and near relatives in kindness (equitably). (2:180)

According to Aṭ-Ṭabarī, Allah means by His statement in this verse: It was written for you, i.e., the will was made obligatory on you, O ye believers, when death approaches one of you, if you leave « خير » and « الخير » is "the wealth", to parents and relatives who are not legal inheritors of it, in fairness, that is what Allah allowed with respect to the will. By « حَقّاً عَلىٰ المتّقِينَ » He means that it is obligatory on you, a duty on whoever fears Allah, so obey Him and do it. Thus, if someone asked: Is it obligatory on the man who is the possessor of wealth, that he make a will for his parents and relatives who are not legal inheritors? It is said: Yes. And if he asked: And if he neglects to do that, will he be neglecting a *farḍ* (required duty)? It is said: Yes. Aṭ-Ṭabarī bases his conclusion on the fact that the Qur'ānic text is stated in the same way as the text making fasting obligatory: « كُتِبَ عَلَيْكُمْ الصِّيَامُ » [1] « كُتِبَ عَلَيْكُمْ إذا حَضَرَ » .

Aṭ-Ṭabarī quotes many sources which indicate that after the revelation of Sūrah 4, Verses 11-12, this verse (2:180) makes the will applicable only to those relatives not stipulated in Sūrah 4, Verses 11-12. One such source is Qatādah's statement: Thus, Allah instituted the will for parents and relatives; then, He cancelled that and gave the parents an obligatory fixed share of the inheritance; thus, the will became applicable to those who had relatives that were not legal inheritors, and a will is not permissible for legal inheritors.[2]

As indicated by the previous discussion, mothers and other relatives of the deceased, who are non-Muslims, may be provided for by will, up to one third, to the exclusion of legal heirs. On the other hand, the remaining two thirds of the inheritable wealth of the deceased is to be distributed amongst the Muslim relatives of the deceased, the legal heirs.[3] The Qur'ānic injunction which deals with the inheritance of the mother as legal heir is:

> "And to each of his parents a sixth of the inheritance, if he has a child; and if he has no child and his parents are his heirs, then to his mother one third; and if he has brothers (or sisters) then to his mother the sixth, after the payment of legacies and debts. Your parents and your children: Ye know not which of them is nearer unto you in usefulness." (4:11)

As this verse conclusively determines the share of the mother, there is no *ra'y* (legal opinion). The commentary, thus, rests in clarification of terminology and of the varying circumstances mentioned, and the extended situations which may occur if the mother of the deceased is also deceased.

In the following discussion concerning the Muslim mother as legal heir, it must be remembered that the shares mentioned are considered as fractions of the *total amount remaining* after the termination of funeral expenses, debts and will, and that the existence or lack of existence of various members of the family causes adjustments, up or down, in the amount of the share. The first condition is that she and the father inherit together with the children of the deceased; then, both parents equally get one sixth of what remains of the deceased's wealth. This is regardless to whether the dead person had one child or more. However, as Aṭ-Ṭabarī explains, in the case of someone who dies and has only one daughter, and no other children, there is an increase in the available share because the only daughter's share is one half. In this case, the excess, i.e., above and beyond the stipulated one sixth to each parent, goes to the closest paternal relative to the deceased; thus, the father receives more than the mother. Aṭ-Ṭabarī attributes this decision to the Messenger of Allah (ﷺ) concluding that this is so because the deceased's father in this case is the responsible person, as the deceased did not have a son.[4]

The next condition is when someone dies and has no children. In this case, the mother gets one third of the deceased's remaining wealth as stipulated. But, Aṭ-Ṭabarī says, if someone asked: Then, who gets the other two thirds? It is said: The father gets it because he is the closest paternal relative to the dead person, as the Messenger of Allah (ﷺ) made clear to his followers that the closest paternal relative to the dead person is the first to have a right to his inheritance after the giving to those upon whom shares are obligatory (by Qur'ānic injunction). He adds that due to this right of the father, it is necessary only to clarify the mother's share, as was done in verse 11.[5]

The one third share of the mother, however, may be adjusted downwards as the existence of brothers and sisters affect it. In discussion of this point, it is first necessary to clarify what number the word « إخوة » represents, i.e., a minimum of two or a minimum of three. Although « إخوة » is usually the plural form (three or more persons), in this context it has been traditionally understood as a minimum of two. Thus, Aṭ-Ṭabarī says that a group of the Companions of the Messenger of Allah (ﷺ) and the *tābi'īn* of the *'Ulamā'* of the community of Islam of all times said that Allah meant to refer to two brothers or sisters (as a minimum) i.e., two sisters or more, two brothers or more, or one male and one female.[6] Al-Qurṭubī adds that they could be from the same parents or from the same father only or the same mother, i.e., half-sisters or half-brothers.[7] In connection with this condition, in the case where the deceased has no children, to this, Qatādah says, one brother or sister does not reduce the mother's share, but more than one does, although in this situation, these « إخوة » do not inherit. His clarification is that *Ahl Al-'Ilm* were of the opinion that the « إخوة » prevented the mother from one third, because their father was responsible for their marriage contracts and their support, without depending on the mother.[8]

The next condition is when the mother and father inherit together with only a husband or a wife of the deceased. If it is a husband, he gets one half and if it is a wife, she gets one fourth. In this case, the *'Ulamā'* differ about what the mother gets, the correct ruling of which Ibn Kathīr says is the following. The mother gets one third of the remainder (after the husband or wife) for two reasons: (1) because it is as if it is the entire inheritance with respect to the parents, and (2) because Allah has provided for the mother one half of what He has provided for the father; thus, she gets one third and the father the remaining two thirds. He says this is the statement of 'Umar and 'Uthmān and it is confirmed by 'Alī, and that Ibn Mas'ūd and Zaid Ibn Thābit use it, and it is the statement of *Al-Fuqahā' As-Sab'ah* and the four *Imāms* (Abū Ḥanīfah, Ash-Shāfi'ī, Mālik and Ibn Ḥanbal) and the majority of the *'Ulamā'*.[9]

Based on the concept of *ḥirmān* (the process of exclusion from inheritance based on degrees of closeness of relationship to the deceased), grandmothers do not inherit if the mother of the deceased is still alive, according to *Ahl Al-'Ilm*. If, however, the mother is dead, then they all agree that the category of grandmother inherits the mother's share. Within this agreement, however, there are points of disagreement. The following diagram will be used to clarify the discussion about the points of disagreement.

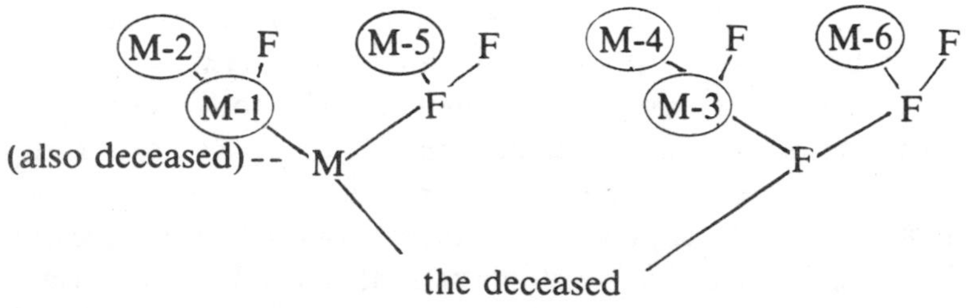

Al-Qurṭubī includes the ensuing explication of this matter, which proceeds under the assumption that the mother of the deceased is also dead.[10] There is agreement that the existence of the father of the deceased does not prevent the grandmother (M-1) from inheriting. But, *Ahl Al-'Ilm* disagree as to whether the grandmother (M-3) inherits if her son is still alive. Thus, that the grandmother does not inherit if her son is still alive has been stated by Zaid Ibn Thābit and 'Uthmān and 'Alī. And it is used by Mālik, Ath-Thaurī, Al-'Uwzā'ī, Abū Thaur and *Aṣḥāb Ar-Ra'y*. On the other hand, it is related that 'Uthmān and 'Alī have also said that the grandmother inherits together with her son, as has been said by 'Amr Ibn Mas'ūd and Ibn Mūsā. And it has been used by Shuraiḥ, Jābir Ibn Zaid, 'Ubaid Allah Ibn Al-Ḥasan, Shurīk, Aḥmad Ibn Ḥanbal, Isḥāq and Ibn Mundhur. Accordingly, At-Tirmidhī reports on the authority of 'Abdullah that the Messenger of Allah (ﷺ) provided the first grandmother (in Islam) with support of one sixth together with her living son.[11]

In addition, although the four *Imāms* agree on the fact that the category of grandmother inherits in case the mother is also deceased, there is disagreement about which of the grandmothers becomes the legal heir. Mālik and the people of Madīnah and Zaid Ibn Thābit said that only two categories of grandmothers can inherit: the mothers of the mother of the deceased and the mothers of the father, i.e., (M-1), (M-2), (M-3) and (M-4) can inherit, while (M-5) and (M-6) cannot. Abū Thaur also attributes this to Ash-Shāfi'ī, and a group of the *tābi'īn* have used it. This varies according to circumstance; thus, Mālik says that if only one grandmother of these two categories is alive, she gets the full one sixth. But, if both categories inherit together, and are of the same degree of closeness, i.e., (M-1) and (M-3); then, one sixth is shared between them. If on the other hand, one is closer than the other, and the closest is from the mother's side (M-1); then, she gets one sixth and (M-4) does not inherit. But, if it is a case of (M-2) and (M-3), where the closest relationship is on the father's side; then the one sixth is shared between them. Also, (M-1) and (M-2) cannot inherit together, the closer grandmother (M-1) having the preference. Thus, from Mālik's rulings, it can be seen that he gives preference to the grandmothers on the mother's side as substitute heirs for the mother. However, Aḥmad Ibn Ḥanbal says that three grandmothers inherit together, one from the mother's side, i.e., (M-1) or (M-2), and two from the father's side i.e., (M-3) and (M-4), thus giving preference to the father's line of kinship. Abū Ḥanīfah and Ath-Thaurī say that the inheritance goes to the closest of the grandmothers, whether from the mother's side or the father's side, i.e., (M-1) or (M-3), giving no preference to either, the concern being the closeness of the relationship to the deceased.

Contained in verse 11 is the reason for the insistence on precision in the carrying out of inheritance laws in Islam: « آباؤُكُمْ وأَبْناؤُكُمْ ... أقْربُ لَكُمْ نَفْعاً ». Thus, Aṭ-Ṭabarī says the meaning is: Give your parents and your children their due of the inheritance, as you do not know which of them is closer and more beneficial to you in your present lifetime and in your appointed Afterlife. In reference to the Hereafter, Ibn 'Abbās said: Obey Allah with reference to parents and children and this will raise you up a degree on the Day of Resurrection because Allah, May He Be Praised, lets the believers plead on each other's behalf.[12] Al-Qurṭubī says in reference to this world, the meaning is by *du'ā'* (prayer for parents) and *ṣadaqah* (charity to parents), and thereby includes the following Ḥadīth:

« حدثنا يَحْيى بنُ أيّوبَ وقُتَيْبَةُ – يعنى ابنَ سعيد – وابنُ حُجرٍ قالوا حدثنا إسماعيل – وهو ابنُ جعفر – عن العلاء عن أبيه عن أبي هريرةَ أنّ رسول الله ﷺ قال إذا مات الإنْسانُ انقطَعَ عنْهُ عَمَلُهُ إلّا من ثلاثةٍ إلّا من صَدَقَةٍ جاريةٍ أو عِلْمٍ يُنْتَفَعُ بِهِ أو وَلَدٍ صالح يَدْعُو لَهُ » .

> "Narrated Abū Hurairah (رضى) that the Messenger of Allah (ﷺ) said: When a human being dies, his good works are ended, except in three cases: except through a continuing charity (i.e., *al-waqf,)* or knowledge from which one can benefit, or a good child through his prayers for his parent." (Muslim)[13]

In summary, Qur'ānic injunction establishes that a share of the inheritance is legally due to the Muslim mother of the deceased, although the exact portion varies accordingly, under specified circumstances. Further, in accordance with *ḥirmān,* the grandmother attains inheritance status only in lieu of the mother, and the precise application of the principle varies amongst the Four Schools. In addition, Islam allows for the inclusion of non-Muslim mothers in the inheritance by way of a specified will, which may amount to one third of the deceased's wealth after preliminary expenses are concluded, and the writing of such will is even considered to be *farḍ* amongst some of the *'Ulamā'*.

NOTES

[1]Aṭ-Ṭabarī, v. 2, pp. 115-116. Also see Ibn Kathīr, v. 1, p. 213 and *Ṣaḥīḥ Al-Bukhārī,* v. 4, Kitāb Al-Waṣāya, p. 1 for Ḥadīth supporting this conclusion. For a counter opinion, see Al-Qurṭubī, v. 2, p. 260 and p. 267 on whether the will is *farḍ* or *nadab* (recommended).

[2]Aṭ-Ṭabarī, v. 2, pp. 116-117. Also, the making of a will for a legal heir is allowed by some of the *'Ulamā',* on condition that the other legal heirs agree. See Al-Qurṭubī, v. 2, p. 265.

[3]See *Ṣaḥīḥ Al-Bukhārī,* v. 8, Kitāb Al-Farā'iḍ, p. 498 for Ḥadīth defining legal heirs. Also, Muḥammad Ibn 'Alī Ibn Muḥammad Ash-Shawkānī, *Nail Al-Awṭār* (Cairo: Idārat Aṭ-Ṭab'ah Al-Munīrah, 1925) v. 6, p. 192-194 for his discussion of the legality or illegality of inheritance of Muslims with non-Muslims.

[4]Aṭ-Ṭabarī, v. 4, p. 277.

[5]Ibid.

[6]Aṭ-Ṭabarī, v. 4, p. 278. Also, see Ibn Kathīr, v. 1, p. 459 for the discussion between Ibn 'Abbās (رضى) and 'Uthmān (رضى) of this point.

[7]Aṭ-Qurṭubī, v. 5, p. 72.

[8]Aṭ-Ṭabarī, v. 4, p. 280.

[9]Ibn Kathīr, v. 1, p. 458.

[10]Al-Qurṭubī, v. 5, pp. 70-71.

[11]Al-Qurṭubī, v. 5, p. 70.

[12]Aṭ-Ṭabarī, v. 4, p. 281.

[13]*Ṣaḥīḥ Muslim,* v. 11, Kitāb Al-Waṣīyyah, Bāb Wuṣūl Thawāb Aṣ-Ṣadaqāt Ilā Al-Mait, pp. 84-85. Also, Al-Qurṭubī, v. 5, pp. 74-75.

CHAPTER III

JUST BEHAVIOUR AND THE LIMITS TO OBEDIENCE

The Muslim child is commanded to have reverence, respect and concern for his mother, but Islam does not countenance the child's absolute, unconditional freedom to obey his parents. In general, there is freedom, but there are limits to this freedom. There are responsibilities, and there are limits. Witness the mention of "the limits of Allah" fourteen times in the Qur'ān.[1]

The following two verses establish a limit to the obedience due to parents:

> "We have enjoined on man kindness to parents, but if they strive to make thee join with Me that of which thou hast no knowledge; then obey them not." (29:8)

> "But if they (parents) strive to make thee join in worship with Me things of which thou hast no knowledge, obey them not; yet be their companion in this life as well as you can." (31:15)

In discussion of these verses, Aṭ-Ṭabarī gives a literal interpretation of the Qur'ānic text, while Ibn Kathīr specifies that if parents strive to get you to follow them in their religion while they are polytheists, do not obey them in that.[2] Both commentators mention that it is said that these verses were revealed for Sa'd Ibn Abī Waqqāṣ, when he migrated to the Prophet (ﷺ) as a result of the situation described in the following Hadīth:

« حدثنا هناد بن السريّ قال حدثنا أبو الأحوص ، عن سماك بن حرب ، عن مصعب بن سعد ، قال : حلفت أمّ سعد أن لا تأكل ولا تشرب حتى يتحوّل سعد عن دينه ، قال : فأبى عليها فلم تزل كذلك حتى غشي عليها ، قال : فأتاها بنوها فسقوها ، قال : فلما أفاقت دعت الله عليه ، فنزلت هذه الآية » .

"Narrated Mus'ab Ibn Sa'd: He said: The mother of Sa'd swore that she would not eat or drink until Sa'd renounced his religion. He said: But, I refused her, and this continued until she fainted. He said: And then, her son came to her and gave her drink. He said: And when she regained consciousness, she cursed him;, then, this verse was revealed."[3]

Al-Qurṭubī separates the two verses, mentioning other possible reasons, as well as the above-mentioned reason, for the revelation of Sūrah 29, Verse 8, one of which is that it was revealed for the early community of Islam when they were not patient during Allah's testing of them with suffering at the hands of the non-believers.[4] He saves his unreserved statement that the verse was revealed for Sa'd and his mother, who was Ḥamnah bint Abī Sufyān Ibn Ḥarb Ibn 'Umayyah, for Sūrah 31:14-15.[5]

In specifying the meaning of Sūrah 31, Verse 15, Ibn Kathīr adds that even though the Muslim must not succumb to non-believing parents, trying to pull him away from his religion, that does not prevent him from befriending them in this world as best he can, i.e., in kindness to them.[6] In further clarifying what this verse allows, Al-Qurṭubī says it points to the granting of what is possible of one's wealth to the non-believing parents, if they are poor, and also to gentleness of speech and *du'ā'* in order to bring them to Islam in a kind, friendly spirit.[7] As to what is not allowed, he says that obedience to parents does not include heeding them in committing a major sin or neglecting to do « فريضة على الأعيان » (duties that are *farḍ* for each individual). Obedience to them is required in matters that are « المباحات »(allowed in Islamic law), and it is acceptable to put aside duties that are « الطاعات الندب »(specifically assigned), an example of which is the command of *jihād,* which is« الكفاية »(a *farḍ* for a specific limited number of unspecified people). He adds that the request of the mother while one is praying, if he has the possibility to return to his prayer, on the basis that the request is stronger than« الندب »is justified if he fears she is in danger, or in conditions similar to those which allow the breaking of prayer; otherwise, the request is not stronger than « الندب ». Al-Ḥasan disagrees with this point saying that if his mother prevents him from making the *'Ishā'* prayer solicitously, he must not obey her.[8]

The following verse establishes the limits placed on the Muslim with respect to a conflict of affection for the mother and respect for Allah's command to be just under all circumstances:

> "O ye who believe! Be staunch in justice, witnesses for Allah, even though it be against yourselves or (your) parents or (your) kindred, whether (the case be of) a rich man or a poor man, for Allah can best protect both." (4:135)

Both Aṭ-Ṭabarī and Ibn Kathīr confirm that this verse was revealed for the believers generally. All three commentators agree about the intended meaning of the verse, while Aṭ-Ṭabarī devotes some discussion to its ramifications with reference to the rich and the poor, and Al-Qurṭubī gives further clarification about the acceptance of testimony.

Aṭ-Ṭabarī states that the meaning is: Be absolutely correct and just to Allah in the matter of your testimony, even if it is against yourself or your parents or your relatives, such that you persist and state the truth. And do not favour, in your testimony, the rich because of his wealth, nor the poor because of his poverty, and thus commit injustice, for it is Allah who decides between the case of the rich and that of the poor justly, protecting them. And He has more right than you do because He is their Sovereign and Protector, thus, He knows wherein their best interests lie. Therefore, He commanded you to be just in your testimony for them or against them. Then, Aṭ-Ṭabarī asks the rhetorical questions: And if someone asked: How can one give testimony against himself justly? And does one witness against himself? He answers saying: It is said: "Yes". And that is when someone else is in the right against him; then, he decides in the other person's favour, and that is giving testimony against himself.[9]

Aṭ-Ṭabarī, Ibn 'Abbās, Ibn Shahāb and Qatādah agree that

this verse was revealed as a lesson from Allah to the believers that they do as did those who absolved Banī Abīriq from stealing and plotting, as described in the following Ḥadīth:

« من ذكر ماقيل عند رسول آلله ﷺ ، وشهادتهم لهم عنده بالصلاح ، فقال لهم : إذا قمتم بالشهادة لإنسان أو عليه ، فقوموا فيها بالعدل ، ولو كانت شهادتكم على أنفسكم أو على آبائكم أو على أمهاتكم أو على أقربائكم ، فلا يحملنكم غنى من شهدتم له أو فقره أو قرابته ورحمة منكم على الشهادة له بالزور ولا على ترك الشهادة عليه بالحقّ وكتمانها » .

> "From the report of what was said in the presence of the Messenger of Allah (ﷺ) and their (the believers') witness for them (Banī Abīriq) to him (the Prophet (ﷺ)) desiring to correct the situation. So, he (the Prophet (ﷺ)) said to them: If you give testimony for someone or against him then give it with justness, even if your testimony is against yourselves or your fathers or your mothers or your relatives. And do not let wealth change your testimony in favour of him, or poverty or familial relationships, and make you merciful towards him, so that you testify in his favour with false testimony, or you neglect to testify against him with the truth and instead suppress it."[10]

Ibn Kathīr says, in other words, give your testimony desiring the presence of Allah because at that time (when you face Allah), the correctness of the situation, about which you gave testimony, will be truly represented, free of distortion, falsification or suppressed evidence. He adds that if the testimony is against your parents and relatives, not to be afraid of them in it, rather testify to the truth even though harm may come to them.[11] Al-Qurṭubī carries this a step further, saying that although the testimony of a child against his parents is decisively approved, this does not imply lack of kindness to them, rather kindness to them is that he testifies against them and stops them from doing wrong.[12] This he says, is the meaning of the Most High's statement:

"O ye who believe! Save yourselves and your families from the Fire." (66:6)

Al-Qurṭubī further states that the word « قَوَّامِين » is a construction of exaggeration « بناء مبالغه » in order to emphasize the point of being just and truthful in all cases, due to human weakness in the face of family ties, money affairs, etc. Because of these human constraints, the testimony of those concerned in such relationships is not acceptable unless the witness is « عدل » i.e., a person having a good reputation as being just and fair in all matters, but the circumstances under which this condition is imposed and on whom varies amongst the *'Ulamā'*. In effect, this difference of opinion has come about because as people changed, the attitude of the law changed. According to Ibn Shahāb Az-Zuhrī's statement, in the past, amongst the upright ancestors, they allowed the testimony of parents and brothers, based on Sūrah 4, Verse 135, and there was no one who doubted the testimony. Then, amongst the people, there appeared matters causing them to be doubted, so the testimony of those who were doubted was disregarded, and this led to not allowing the testimony of the child, the parent, the sibling, the husband and the wife, unless they were classified as « عدولا » (persons of good reputation). This, with some specifications, is the school of Al-Ḥasan, An-Nakha'ī, Ash-Sha'bī, Shurīkh, Mālik, Ath-Thaurī, Ash-Shāfi'ī and Ibn Ḥanbal. It is related that 'Umar Ibn Al-Khaṭṭāb (رضى) and 'Umar Ibn 'Abd Al-Azīz (رضى) accepted this view, and Isḥāq, Ath-Thaurī and Mazanī use it. It is related that Ibn Wahāb does not allow testimony if it involves the witness's child or his share of wealth from an inheritance. Abū Ḥanīfah does not accept the testimony of a husband in favour of his wife because of the nature of their relationship. Ash-Shāfi'ī, on the other hand, allows the testimony of husband and wife, each for the other, because they are not blood relatives.[13]

In summary, if a Muslim's mother encourages her child to fulfil the *farḍ* responsibilities, if she serves to buttress his faith and religious practice, there is no limit to the child's requirement of obedience. On the other hand, nothing and no one must be allowed to destroy one's faith and correct exercise of religious obligations, most pointedly that of truthful testimony. Consequently, if the child feels he would be compromising his call to be fair and just or his fulfilment of a duty to Allah by complying with his mother's desires, he must not let his natural affection for her overcome him. Thus are the limits set by Allah. It is to be kept in mind, however, that even under such strained circumstances, the Muslim child is required to exercise the greatest tact, kindness, respect and concern, both financially and otherwise, for his mother, be she Muslim or non-Muslim.

NOTES

[1]Muḥammad Fu'ād Abd Al-Bāqī, *Al-Mu'jam Al-Mufahras Li Alfāẓ Al-Qur'ān Al-Karīm* (Beirut: Mu'assasah Jamāl Li An-Nashr), p. 195. See references to « حدود » and « حدوده ».

[2]Aṭ-Ṭabarī, v. 20, p. 131. Ibn Kathīr, v. 3, p. 405.

[3]Aṭ-Ṭabarī, op. cit. and v. 21, p. 70. Ibn Kathīr states that similar versions of this Ḥadīth are reported by At-Tirmidhī, Aḥmad, Muslim and Abū Dāwūd, v. 3, p. 405.

[4]Al-Qurṭubī, v. 13, p. 328.

[5]Ibid., v. 14, p. 65.

[6]Ibn Kathīr, v. 3, p. 445.

[7]Al-Qurṭubī, v. 14, p. 65.

[8]Ibid., v. 14, p. 63.

[9]Aṭ-Ṭabarī, v. 5, p. 321.

[10]Aṭ-Ṭabarī, v. 5, p. 321.

[11]Ibn Kathīr, v. 1, p. 565.

[12]Al-Qurṭubī, v. 5, p. 410.

[13]Al-Qurṭubī, v. 5, pp. 410-411.

PART II

THE PERSPECTIVE OF THE MOTHER TOWARDS THE CHILD

CHAPTER IV

CHARACTERISTICS OF THE MOTHER

The mother in Islam is placed in a lofty position, that of the greatest respect, but this does not occur in a vacuum. It involves her active participation in the affairs of her family. In Islam, there are two aspects of the characteristics of the mother: that which aligns itself to responsibility, and that which is attributed to natural, God-given qualities, including both the physical exertion of childbirth[1] and the expression of positive emotion. These two aspects are not mutually exclusive, but rather supportive of each other, thus buttressing a state of equilibrium which is the desired atmosphere in the Muslim household.

« حدثنا عبدان : أخبرنا عبد آللّٰه : أخبرنا موسى بن عُقْبَة ، عن نافع ، عن ابن عُمَر رضى آللّٰه عنهما ، عن النبى ﷺ قال : كلكم مَسْؤُولٌ عن رعيتِهِ والأميرُ راعٍ والرجلُ راعٍ على أهل بيتِهِ . والمرأةُ راعيةٌ على بيت زوجها وولدِهِ . فكلكم راعٍ وكلكم مسؤولٌ عن رعيتِهِ » .

> "Narrated Ibn 'Umar (رضى): The Prophet (ﷺ) said: Each of you is a guardian and is responsible for his ward. The ruler is a guardian and the man is a guardian of the members of his household; and the woman is a guardian and is responsible for her husband's house and his offspring; and so each of you is a guardian and is responsible for his ward." (Al-Bukhārī and Muslim)[2]

The two emotional characteristics of the mother singled out by Ḥadīth are affection and generosity. A mother's affection for her children is considered a normal emotion and a blessing from Allah:

« حدثنا ابن نُميرٍ حدثنا أبو معاوية عن داود بن أبى هند عن أبى عثمان عن

سلمان ، قال قال رسول آلله ﷺ إنَّ آلله خَلَقَ يَوْمَ خَلَقَ السَّمٰوٰاتِ والأرض مائة رَحْمَةٍ كل رحمةٍ طباق مابين السّماء والأرض فجعل منها فى الأرض رحمة بها تَعْطِفُ الوالدةُ على ولدِها » .

(From a longer Ḥadīth): "Salmān reported that Allah's Messenger (ﷺ) said: Verily, Allah created on the same day when He created the heavens and the earth, one hundred parts of mercy. Every part of mercy is analagous to the space between the heavens and the earth, and He out of this mercy endowed one part to the earth and it is because of this that the mother shows affection to her child." (Muslim)[3]

Thus, it follows logically that a woman who does not feel affection for her children is exhibiting abnormal behaviour, according to Islamic thought. In addition, the exhibition of such affection is a characteristic which endears her to her husband, thus strengthening the bond between the members of the family unit.

From a longer Ḥadīth:

« ومايعجبك منها ، لقد رَحِمها آلله برحمتها صبيَّتها » (الحاكم – عن أنس) .

"Narrated Anas: And what pleases you about her. Allah has blessed her with mercy for her children." (Al-Ḥākim)[4]

The second of these characteristics is generosity, i.e., the opposite of selfishness. Generosity can be expressed in many ways – in terms of a willingness to give one's time to one's children or to share knowledge or to give assistance when needed. This may even include financial aid in a situation where the father is poor or incapacitated, and the mother has wealth or income of her own. Besides the immediate gratifications of such generosity, there is Allah's promise of compensation in the Hereafter, as indicated in the following Ḥadīths:

« حدثنا أبو اليمان : أخبرنا شُعَيْبٌ عن الزهرى قال : حدثنى عبد آلله بن أبى

بكر : أن عَرْوَة بن الزبير أخبره : أن عائشة زوج النبى ﷺ حدثته قالت : جاءتنى امرأةٌ معها ابنتان تسألُنى فلم تجد عندى غير تمرةٍ واحدةٍ فأعطيتُها فقسمتْها بين ابنتيْها ، ثم قامت فخرجتْ ، فدخل النّبى ﷺ فحدثتهُ فقال : من يلى من هذه البناتِ شيئاً فأَحْسَنَ إليهنّ كنَّ لهُ ستراً من النار» .

"Narrated 'Ā'isha (رضى) the wife of the Prophet (ﷺ): A lady along with her two daughters came to me asking for alms, but she did not find anything with me except one date, which I gave to her and she divided it between her two daughters, and got up and went away. Then, the Prophet (ﷺ) came in and I informed him of this story. He said: Whoever is in charge of these daughters and treats them generously, then, they will act as a shield for him from the Fire. (Al-Bukhārī, Muslim and At-Tirmidhī)[5]

« حدثنا أبو كريب محمد بن العلاء حدثنا أبو أُسامة حدثنا هشام عن أبيه عن زينب بنت أبى سلمة عن أُمّ سلمة قالت قلْتُ يارسول آلله هل لى أجرٌ فى بنى أبى سلمة أُنْفِقُ عليهم ولسْتُ بتارِكتهم هكذا إنما هم بنىَّ فقال نعم لك فيهم أجْرُ ما أنفقْتِ عليهم » .

"Narrated Umm Sallamah: I asked the Messenger of Allah (ﷺ) whether there is a reward for me if I spend on Abū Sallamah's sons, and I am not for abandoning them in this state of helplessness, for they are my sons. He said: Yes, for you there is the reward for what you spend on them." (Muslim and Al-Bukhārī)[6]

«رَيْطة بنت عبد آلله امراة عبد آللهبن مسعود وأم ولده ، وكانت امراة صناعاً . فقالت : يارسول آللهإنى امرأة ذات صنعة أبيع منها وليس لى ولا لزوجى ولا لولدى شىء ، وسألته عن النفقة عليهم فقال : لك فى ذلك أجر ما أنفقت عليهم» .

"Narrated Raiṭah bint 'Abdullah, the wife of 'Abdullah Ibn Mas'ūd and the mother of his child. And she was a craftswoman. So, she said: O Messenger of Allah (ﷺ) I am a woman who is an artisan and I sell what I make. And neither my husband nor my son have anything (i.e., wealth). And she asked him about spending on them. He said: In doing that there is a reward for you equal to what you spend on them."[7]

In summary, the Muslim mother has a distinctive role to play in the day-to-day operations of the family. Her role is basic and necessary to the harmonious atmosphere amongst its members. In order to carry out this responsibility, she needs good health, in addition to general and religious knowledge. Above all, the ideal Muslim mother is affectionate and kind to her children, often placing their needs before her own, thereby gaining Allah's reward for her generosity.

NOTES

[1]Both childbirth and child rearing will be discussed in detail in Chapter V.

[2]*Ṣaḥīḥ Al-Bukhārī,* v. 7, Kitāb An-Nikāḥ, p. 98. Also, *Riyāḍ Aṣ-Ṣāliḥīn,* Bāb Ḥaqq Az-Zauj 'Alā Al-Mar'ah, p. 95.

[3]*Ṣaḥīḥ Muslim,* v. 17, Kitāb At-Tawbah, Bāb Sā'ah Raḥmat Allah Ta'ālā Wa Annaha Taghlib Ghadbahu, p. 69.

[4]*Kanz,* v.16, p. 459 (No. 45428).

[5]*Ṣaḥīḥ Al-Bukhārī,* v. 8, Kitāb Al-Adab, p. 17. Also, Khān, Bāb Mā Warada Fī Birr Al-Awlād Wa Al-Aqārib, pp. 237-238.

[6]*Ṣaḥīḥ Muslim,* v. 7, Kitāb Az-Zakāt, Bāb Faḍl An-Nafaqah Wa Aṣ-Ṣadaqah 'Alā Al-Aqrabīn Wa Az-Zauj Wa Al-Awlād, p. 88. Also, *Riyāḍ Aṣ-Ṣāliḥīn,* Bāb An-Nafaqah 'Alā Al-'Ayāl, p. 96.

[7]Muḥammad Ibn Sa'd, *Aṭ-Ṭabaqāt Al-Kubrā* (Beirut: Dār Ṣādir) v. 8, Kitāb Fī An-Nisā', p. 290.

CHAPTER V

PREGNANCY, CHILDBIRTH, NURSING AND REARING[1]

From the Islamic point of view, marriage is the desired state of affairs:

« إذا تزوج العبدُ فقد استكملَ نصف الدين ، فليتق ٱللّٰه فى النصف الباقى» .
(احمد – عن أنس) .

> "Narrated Anas: If the slave (of Allah) marries, he has completed half of the Religion; so let him fear Allah (through worship and service) with the remaining half." (Aḥmad)[2]

and childbirth is considered the natural outcome of marriage. The Muslim woman sees pregnancy, childbirth, nursing and rearing as a spiritual act. It is her exclusive opportunity to obtain Allah's blessings and rewards, as the difficulty of pregnancy and childbirth is a way which Allah has allotted only to the female sex. On one hand, she has been endowed with suitable characteristics for the task, and on the other, she is to be rewarded for her efforts by her children. Thus, even if she does no more than simply bring them into this world, they are bound, as Muslims, to respect and have concern for her. The following two Qur'ānic verses clearly indicate the obligation on the Muslim of reverence to the mother because of her child-bearing responsibilities:

> "And We have enjoined upon man concerning his parents – His mother beareth him in weakness upon weakness, and his weaning is in two years – Give thanks unto Me and unto thy parents. Unto Me is the journeying." (31:14)

> "And We have enjoined on man kindness toward parents.

His mother beareth him with reluctance, and bringeth him forth with reluctance, and the bearing of him and the weaning of him is thirty months, till, when he attaineth full strength and reacheth forty years, he saith: My Lord: Arouse me that I may give thanks for the favour wherewith Thou has favoured me and my parents, and that I may do right acceptable unto Thee. And be gracious unto me in the matter of my seed." (46:15)

The phrase « وَهْناً عَلَىٰ وَهْنٍ » found in Sūrah 31, Verse 14, which has been translated as "weakness upon weakness" has a fuller meaning, which the commentators have attempted to describe. Aṭ-Ṭabarī says it means weakness upon weakness, and straining upon straining. Qatādah says it is effort upon effort; and thus Ibn Kathīr comments that the Most High mentions the mother's rearing of the child and tiring herself, and her hardship staying awake night and day, in order to remind the child of her previous kindness to him. Al-Qurṭubī says it refers to the period in which she carried him in pregnancy, and she increased each day in weakness upon weakness. Muḥammad Ṣiddīq Khān summarizes in his statement: It is said that pregnancy is « وهن », the labour pains are « وهن » and the delivery is « وهن » and the nursing is « وهن ».[3] Then, in reference to « إِلَيَّ المصيرُ » Ibn Kathīr says that the meaning is that Allah will give an abundant reward for giving thanks to your parents.[4] Sufyān Ibn 'Uyainah adds that he who prays the five prayers has thereby given thanks to Allah, the Most High, and he who makes *du'ā'* for his parents after his prayers has thereby given thanks to them.[5]

The Ḥadīth explains the importance of the mother's task and the great reward she receives:

« عن أنس رضى الله عنه : أن سلامة حاضنة إبراهيم بن النبى ﷺ قالت : يارسول الله تبشر الرجال بكل خير ولا تبشر النساء ، قال : أصويحباتك دسسنك لهذا ؟ قالت : أجل هن أمرننى ، قال : أفما ترضى إحداكن أنها إذا كانت حاملا من زوجها وهو عنها راضى أن لها مثل أجر الصائم القائم فى سبيل الله ، فإذا أصابها الطلق لم يعلم أهل السماء وأهل الأرض ما أخفى لها من قرة أعين ، فإذا وضعت لم يخرج منها جرعة من لبنها ولم يمص مصة إلا كان لها بكل جرعة وبكل مصة حسنة ، فإن

أسهرها ليلة كان لها مثل أجر سبعين رقبة تعتقهن فى سبيل آلله » .

"Narrated Anas (رضى): Sallāmah, the nurse of his son Ibrāhīm, said to the Prophet (ﷺ): O Messenger of Allah, you brought tidings of all the good things to men but not to women. He said: Did your women friends put you up to asking me this question? She said: Yes, they did. He said: Does it not please any one of you that if she is pregnant by her husband and he is satisfied with her that she receives the reward of one who fasts and prays for the sake of Allah? And when the labour pains come no one in Heaven or earth knows what is concealed in her womb to soothe her (to cool her eyes). And when she delivers, not a mouthful of milk flows from her and not an instance of the child's suck, but that she receives, for every mouthful and for every suck, the reward of one good deed. And if she is kept awake by her child at night, she receives the reward of one who frees seventy slaves for the sake of Allah." (Aṭ-Ṭabarānī)[6]

Because of the strong bond of affection that accompanies the great effort of the mother, the loss of children is a heavy burden, but if she accepts it as Allah's will, her reward is Paradise:

« عن عبد الرحمٰن بن الأصبهانى عن أبى صالح ذكوان عن أبى سعيد الُخدْرىّ قال قال النساء للنبى ﷺ : يارسول آلله غلبنا عليك الرجال فاجعل لنا يوماً من نفسك ، فوعدهن يوماً فوعظهن وأمرهن ، وكان فيما قال لهن : مامنكن امرأة تقدم ثلاثة من ولدها إلّا كان ذلك لها حجاباً من النار ، فقالت امرأة يارسول آلله واثنين ؟ قال : واثنين » .

"Narrated Abū Sa'īd: The women said to the Prophet (ﷺ): O Messenger of Allah the men have taken all your time from us, so give us a day with you. And he promised them a day. He preached to them and commanded them and amongst what he told them was: There is not one of you that sends forth (in death) three of your children, but that this will protect her from the Fire. So one woman asked: O Messenger of Allah, what about two? He said: And two." (Muslim and Al-Bukhārī)[7]

« لا يموتُ لِاحداكُنّ ثلاثةٌ من الولدِ فتحتسبهُ إلّا دَخلَتِ الجنَّة » .

And contained in another Ḥadīth: "Not one of you will have three children to die and accept it, (as the will of Allah), but that she will enter Paradise." Then he said: "Or two." (Muslim)[8]

Finally, if the mother dies in childbirth, she is equal to the martyr who dies fighting in the cause of Allah:[9]

« عن عبادة بن الصامت فى حديث طويل (وفى النفساء يقتلها وولدها جمعا شهادة) » .

"Narrated 'Ubādah Ibn Aṣ-Ṣāmit (in a longer Ḥadīth): A woman who dies in childbirth together with the baby, becomes a martyr." (Aḥmad and Aṭ-Ṭabarānī)[10]

In the subsequent verse (46:15), the word« كرها » has been translated as "with reluctance". To further clarify it, Aṭ-Ṭabarī refers to the statements of Mujāhid, Al-Ḥasan and Qatādah that« كرها »means hardship, labour and trouble. He goes on, in his interpretation of the verse, to say that the age of forty years is when Allah has given man matureness and competence; the folly of youth has passed and he knows his duties to Allah of what is right in terms of respect to his parents.[11] Thus, Aṭ-Ṭabarī indicates that a human being does not reach the state of full awareness of his mother's great efforts exerted on his behalf, until he or she has fully experienced the stage of parenthood himself.

Both Aṭ-Ṭabarī and Al-Qurṭubī mention that the verse (46:15) was revealed for Abū Bakr Aṣ-Ṣiddīq (رضى) . According to 'Alī (رضى) both of Abū Bakr's parents became Muslims, and this did not happen in any of the families of the *Muhājirīn,* except that of Abū Bakr; thus, Allah advised him about his parents, and this became obligatory on all Muslims afterwards.

The end of the verse means: Make my descendents pious; make them successful in doing good works that You may be satisfied with them.[12] This provides a guideline for the mother in her responsibility of rearing her children. The Ḥadīths clarify her role of providing her children with religious knowledge, piety, good conduct and morals. In addition, a mother must discipline her children and teach them obedience. At the same time, she should be a good companion to them – sharing and understanding – and generous. One very important factor in child-rearing is the equal treatment of children.

« روى الحاكم عن أبى النضر الفقيه حدثنا محمد بن (حموية)[13] حدثنا أبى حدثنا النضر ابن محمد عن الثورى عن إبراهيم بن مهاجر عن عكرمة حدثنا ابن عباس عن النبى عليه الصلاة والسّلام قال : افتحوا على صبيانكم أول كلمة (ب) لا إله إلا آلله ، ولقنوهم عن الموت : لا إله إلا آلله » .

"Narrated Ibn 'Abbās that the Prophet (ﷺ) said: Pronounce as the first words to your children, 'There is no God but Allah', and recite to them at death, 'There is no God but Allah'." (Al-Ḥākim)[14]

« من ربَّى صغيراً حتى يقول : لا إله إلا آلله لم يحاسبه آلله » (الطبرانى فى الأوسط ، ابن عدى – عن عائشة) .

"Narrated 'Ā'ishah: Whoever brings up a small child until he says 'There is no God but Allah', Allah will not call to account." (Aṭ-Ṭabarānī in *Al-Awsaṭ*; Ibn 'Addī)[15]

« ماورَّث والدٌ ولدَه أفضل من أدبٍ » (العسكرىِ وابن النجار عن ابن عمر) .

"Narrated Ibn 'Umar: What does a parent leave as an inheritance for his child (that is) better than good morals?" (Al-'Askarī and Ibn An-Najjār)[16]

« أكرموا أولادكم ، وأحسنوا آدابهم » (ابن ماجة – عن أنس) .

"Narrated Anas: Be generous to your children, and excel in teaching them the best of conduct." (Ibn Mājah)[17]

« مامن مسلم تُدركُ له ابنتان فيحسنُ إليهما ما صحبتا ، إلا آدخلتاه الجنة » (أحمد ، البخارى فى الأدب ، والخرائطى فى مكارم الأخلاق ، الحاكم ، ابن حبان – عن ابن عباس) .

"Narrated Ibn 'Abbās: There is no Muslim, whose two daughters reach the age (of maturity), and he is good to them as a companion, and they do not cause him to enter Paradise." (Aḥmad; Al-Bukhārī in *Al-Adab*; Al-Kharā'iṭī in *Makārim Al-Akhlāq*; Al-Ḥākim; Ibn Ḥibbān)[18]

« أعينوا أولادكم على البّر ، من شاءَ استخرج العقوق من ولده » (الطبرانى فى الأوسط – عن أبى هريرة) .

"Narrated Abū Hurairah: Set your children's eyes on piety; whoever wants to can purge disobedience from his child." (Aṭ-Ṭabarānī in *Al-Awsaṭ*)[19]

« لأن يؤدب أحدكم ولده خيرٌ له من أن يصدق كل يوم بنصف صاع على مسكين » (الطبرانى فى الكبير ، الحاكم – عن جابر بن سمرة) .

"Narrated Jābir Ibn Samrah: That one of you disciplines his child is better for him than if he gives charity everyday half a *ṣā'* (cubic measure) to a poor person." (Aṭ-Ṭabarānī in *Al-Kabīr*; Al-Ḥākim)[20]

Ibn Al-Qayyim discusses the matter of obedience in the context of explaining the meaning of: "O ye who believe! Save yourselves and your families from a Fire." (66:6). He includes a statement of 'Alī (رضى): "Teach them and train them in good conduct", and another of Al-Ḥasan: "Command them with obedience to Allah and teach them what is good". Then, he mentions the following Ḥadīth, which he says describes three kinds of moral conduct:

« فى المسند وسنن أبى داود من حديث عمرو بن شعيب عن أبيه عن جده ، قال قال رسول الله ﷺ : مروا أبناءكم بالصلاة لسبع ، واضربوهم عليها لعشر ، وفرقوا

بينهم فى المضاجع » .

"From the Ḥadīth of 'Amr Ibn Shu'aib on the authority of his father, on the authority of his grandfather, he said: The Messenger of Allah (ﷺ) said: Order your children to pray at seven, and beat them about it at ten, and in sleeping separate them." (In the *Sunan* of Abū Dāwūd)[21]

The final counsel is that of equal treatment of children:

« اتقوا آلله واعدلوا بين أولادكم » (البخارى ، مسلم – عن النعمان بن بشير) .

From a longer Ḥadīth: "Narrated An-Nu'mān Ibn Bashīr: Fear Allah and treat your children equally." (Al-Bukhārī; Muslim in *Kitāb Al-Hibāt*)[22]

« حدثنا أحمدُ بنُ عبد آلله بن يونُسَ حدثنا زهُيْرٌ حدثنا أبو الزُبَيْر عن جابر قال قالَتْ امرأةُ بشير : انحل ابنى غلامك وأشهد لى رسول آلله ﷺ فأتىٰ رسول آلله ﷺ فقال ابنة فلانٍ سألتنى أن أنحلَ ابنَها غلامى وقالت أشهدْ لى رسول آلله ﷺ فقال : أله إخوةٌ قال نعم قال : أفكلّهم أعطَيتَ مثل ما أعطيتَهُ قال : لا قال : فليس يصلُحُ هذا إنّى لا أشْهدُ إلّا على حقٍ » .

"Narrated Jābir that the wife of Bashīr said: Make a gift of your slave to my son and have the Messenger of Allah (ﷺ) bear witness for me. So he (Bashīr) went to the Messenger of Allah (ﷺ) and said: The daughter of so and so asked that I make a gift of my slave to her son and she said: Have the Messenger of Allah (ﷺ) bear witness for me. Then, he said: Does he have any brothers (or sisters)? He said: Yes. He said: Have you given to each of them like that which you gave to him? He said: No. He said: Then, that is not fair and I do not bear witness except to what is just." (Al-Bukhārī and Muslim)[23]

Ibn Al-Qayyim argues that unequal treatment of children is legally *ḥarām* (forbidden) based on the Prophet's (ﷺ) refusal to bear witness to the act, and the fact that he (ﷺ)

said three times "treat your children equally", thus making it *wujūb* (a required duty).[24]

In summary, although in Islam, there are many ways to open the doors of Paradise, the vehicle especially chosen for the woman is that of pregnancy, childbirth, nursing and conscientious rearing of her children. The commentary clearly points out the great effort and struggle this involves, but for every ounce of effort, be it physical, emotional or mental, exerted in this direction, the mother is elevated to a higher position of esteem in the eyes of her family and society, and has thereby gained a place for herself amongst the successful in the Hereafter.

NOTES

[1]For the legal aspects of nursing and rearing in case of divorce, see Part III.

[2]*Kanz,* v. 16, p. 271 (No. 44403).

[3]Aṭ-Ṭabarī, v. 21, p. 69; Ibn Kathīr, v. 3, p. 445; Al-Qurṭubī, v. 14, p. 64; Khān, Bāb Mā Nazala Fī Muṣāḥibāt Al-Ummahāt Bil-Ma'rūf, p. 159.

[4]Ibn Kathīr, v. 3, p. 445.

[5]Al-Qurṭubī, v. 14, p. 65.

[6]'Abdul Razack, p. 15.

[7]*Ṣaḥīḥ Muslim,* v. 16, Kitāb Al-Birr Wa Aṣ-Ṣilah Wa Al-Adab, Bāb Faḍl Man Yamūtu Lahu Walad Fayaḥtasibuhu, p. 181. ("And it is said: one (child)"), See: Khān, Bāb Mā Warada Fī Man Māta Lahu Thalāthah Min Al-Awlād Aw Ithnān, Aw Wāḥid, p. 471 and p. 392.

[8]*Ṣaḥīḥ Muslim,* op. cit.

[9]See Aḥmad Ghunaim's analysis of this point on pp. 1-2 above.

[10]Khān, Bāb Mā Warada Fī Shahādat An-Nafsā' Wa Makāniha 'Alā Al-Maut, p. 493. Also, according to An-Nawawī, Mālik in the *Muwaṭṭa* includes a Ḥadith that the martyrs are seven, one of which is the mother who dies in childbirth, i.e., together with her child. See, *Ṣaḥīḥ Muslim: Bi Sharḥ An-Nawawī,* v. 13, Kitāb Al-Imārah, Bāb Bayān Ash-Shuhadā', pp. 62-63.

[11]Aṭ-Ṭabarī, v. 16, pp. 15-17.

[12]Al-Qurṭubī, v. 16, p. 194. Also, Aṭ-Ṭabarī, v. 16, p. 17.

[13]Correction:(محمد بن حيوية); see, Aḥmad Ibn 'Alī Ibn Ḥajar Al-'Asqalānī, *Lisān Al-Mīzān* (Al-Hind: Maṭba'ah Dā'irat Al-Ma'ārif An-Niẓāmiyyah, 1331 Heg.) v. 5, p. 151.

[14]Al-Imām Shams Ad-Dīn Muḥammad Ibn Qayyim Al-Jawziyyah, *Tuḥfat Al-Mawdūd Bi Aḥkām Al-Mawlūd* (Cairo: Maktabah Al-Qīmah, 1977) p. 176.

[15]*Kanz,* v. 16, p. 456 (No. 45408).

[16]*Kanz,* v. 16, p. 460 (No. 45435).

[17]Ibid., p. 456 (No. 45410).

[18]Ibid., p. 448 (No. 45370).

[19]*Kanz,* v. 16, p. 457 (No. 45419).

[20]Ibid., p. 461 (No. 45438). Also, Ibn Al-Qayyim, *Tuḥfat,* p. 176.

[21]*Tuḥfat,* p. 176. Also, *Sunan Abū Dāwūd,* v. 1. Kitāb Aṣ-Ṣalāt, Bāb Yu'mar Al-Ghulām Bi Aṣ-Ṣalāt, p. 51.

[22]*Kanz,* v. 16, p. 445 (No. 45353). Also, *Ṣaḥīḥ Muslim,* v. 11 Kitāb Al-Hibāt, Bāb Karāhah Tafḍīl Ba'ḍ Al-Awlād Fī Al-Hibah, p. 67. Also, *Tuḥfat,* p. 178, and in the version included by Ibn Al-Qayyim, "treat your children equally" is repeated three times.

[23]*Ṣaḥīḥ Muslim,* op. cit., v. 11, p. 69, and in another narration, the Messenger of Allah (ﷺ) said: "Then get someone else to bear witness for this." Also, *Riyāḍ Aṣ-Ṣāliḥīn,* Bāb Karāhah Tafḍil Al-Wālid Ba'ḍ Awlādihi, p. 433.

[24]This is also the opinion of Tāwus, 'Urwah, Mujāhid, Ath-Thaurī, Aḥmad, Isḥāq and Dāwūd, see, *Tuḥfat,* pp. 178-179. Also, An-Nawawī adds that this includes equal treatment of both girls and boys. However, he considers a breach of equal treatment *makrūh* (somewhat detested). Concurring with his opinion are Ash-Shāfi'ī, Mālik and Abū Ḥanīfah, see *Sharḥ An-Nawawī,* v. 11, Kitāb Al-Hibāt, pp. 66-67.

CHAPTER VI

LIMITS, MODERATION AND THE EXERCISE OF RELIGIOUS DUTY

By the fulfilment of marriage, and consequent motherhood, the Muslim woman has completed a great part of her religion. The remaining part lies in the obligations incumbent on all adult Muslims, male or female. Although as a wife and mother, she may have to delay such obligations as prayer, for example, in order to attend to urgent needs of her husband or child, she is still held fully responsible for the completion of her religious duties. The following Ḥadīth illustrates the Prophet's (ﷺ) merciful recognition of the conflict that exists between the mother's concern for her child and her desire to fulfil her duty to Allah:

« حدثنا إبراهيمُ بنُ موسىَ قال : أخبرنا الوليد قال : حدثنا الأوزاعِىُّ ، عن يحيى بن أبى كثيرٍ ، عن عبد الله بن أبى قتادة عن أبيه أبى قتادة عن النبى ﷺ قال : إنى لأ قومُ فى الصلاة أريدُ أن أطولَ فيها فأسمعُ بكاءَ الصبىّ فأتجوّزُ فى صلاتى كراهية أن أشق على أمّهِ » .

> "Narrated Abū Qatādah: The Prophet(ﷺ) said: When I stand for prayer, I intend to prolong it, but on hearing the cries of a child, I cut it short, as I dislike to trouble the child's mother." (*Ṣaḥīḥ Al-Bukhārī*)[1]

In spite of the conflict, however, children must not be allowed to hinder the mother from worship of and service to Allah.

The following Qur'ānic verse speaks directly to the point:

> "O ye who believe! Let not your wealth nor your children distract you from remembrance of Allah. Those who do so are the losers." (63:9)

The commentary centres around the meaning of« ذِكْرِ آللَّه ». Ad-Daḥḥāk says, in this case, it means the five prayers. Al-Qurṭubī says that it means the *ḥajj* and *zakāt*, and adds that it is also said to mean the reading of the Qur'ān. According to Al-Ḥasan, it is all of the *farā'iḍ* (obligatory duties), i.e., distraction from obedience to Allah.² In all of these instances, it is easy to see how the mother might become distracted by her children. In the case of *zakāt*, for example, she might become miserly, denying the poor her contribution to their needs by not fulfilling her obligation to them, preferring to spend the money on some unnecessary item for her own children. As the verse indicates, this must be guarded against or she may be beguiled into losing her special share of Allah's blessings and mercy.

The next verse emphasizes the fact that children are « فتنة », i.e., a source of inner turmoil and thus a trial for the believing mother:

> "And know that your possessions and your children are a trial and that with Allah is an immense reward." (8:28)

Ibn Kathīr says, with reference to « فتنة », it is a trial and a test from Allah, such that He gives you children and wealth to see if you will thank Him for them and be obedient to Him, or if you will become preoccupied with them and substitute them for Him. Ibn Kathīr uses the two following Ḥadīths to illustrate the importance of not becoming overly-preoccupied with children and wealth, and also, the inherent struggle involved in doing so:³

« عن أنس رضى آللَّه عنه عن النبيّ ﷺ قال : ثلاثٌ من كنّ فيه وجد بهنّ حلاوة الإيمان : أن يكونَ آللَّه ورسولُهُ أحبَّ إليه ممّا سواهُما ، وأن يُحبَّ المرءَ لا يحبُّهُ إلّا للَّه ، وأن يكره أن يعودَ فى الكفر بعد أن أنقذهُ آللَّه منه كما يكره أن يقذفَ فى النار » .

"Narrated Anas that the Prophet (ﷺ) said: One who possesses the following three things enjoys the sweetness of faith: Allah and His Messenger are more beloved than any other, he loves a human being only out of love for Allah, and he despises returning to non-belief after Allah has saved him from it as much as he despises being thrown into the Fire." (Al-Bukhārī and Muslim)[4]

« حدثنا يعقوبُ بن إبراهيمَ قال : حدثنا ابنُ عُلَيّةَ ، عن عبد العزيز بن صُهَيْبٍ ، عن أنس ، عن النبيّ ﷺ ح وحدثنا آدمُ قال : حدثنا شُعْبَةُ ، عن قتادة ، عن أنس قال : قال النبيّ ﷺ : لا يُؤمن أحدُكم حتّى أكونَ أحبّ إليه من والده وولده والناس اجمعين » .

"Narrated Anas that the Prophet (ﷺ) said: Not one of you believes until I am more beloved to him than his father and child and all the people." (*Ṣaḥīḥ Al-Bukhārī*)[5]

Aṭ-Ṭabarī reminds the believer that no one is unexposed to the kind of *fitnah* mentioned in this verse (8:28). Thus, according to Al-Ḥarith, Ibn Mas'ūd said: There is not amongst you anyone who is not included in *fitnah,* so whoever has been protected from it amongst you, let him ask for Allah's protection from going astray as a result of the trials to come.[6]

The final verse is a warning that the *fitnah* can be so grave that the mother may find herself in a situation such that her family is her enemy:

"O ye who believe! Lo! Among your wives and your children there are enemies for you, therefore beware of them." (64:14)

In his explication of this verse, Al-Qurṭubī says that just as man can have his child and his wife as an enemy, so the woman can have her husband and her child as an enemy. By this meaning, the specific and the general, male and female enter into the interpretation of this verse.[7]

Ibn Kathīr includes the following explanatory Ḥadīth:

« قال الطبرانى حدثنا هاشم بن مرثد حدثنا محمد إسماعيل بن عياش حدثنا أبى حدثنا ضمضم بن زرعة عن شريح بن عبيد عن أبى مالك الأشعرى أن رسول آلله ﷺ قال : ليس عدوك الذى إن قتلته كان فوزا لك وإن قتلك دخلت الجنة ولكن الذى لعله عدو لك ولدك الذى خرج من صلبك ، ثم أعدى عدو لك مالك الذى ملكت يمينك » .

"Narrated Abū Mālik Al-Ash'arī that the Messenger of Allah (ﷺ) said: Your enemy is not the one whom if you

> killed him you would have a reward or if he killed you, you would enter Paradise, but rather the one who perhaps is your enemy is your child who issued forth from your loins; then he makes your wealth which you possessed an enemy to you." (Aṭ-Ṭabarānī)[8]

The *Qāḍī* Abū Bakr Ibn Al-'Arabī further clarifies the meaning of enmity. He says that the enemy is not ipso facto an enemy, rather he is an enemy by virtue of his deeds. Thus, if the spouse and child act as the enemy, they are the enemy, and there is no deed more shameful and repugnant than the separation between the slave (of Allah) and his obedience to Allah.[9]

It is said that this verse was revealed about some men who became Muslims in Makkah and wanted to go on the *hijrah,* but were prevented from doing so by their wives and children. But Allah was merciful to them even though they had previously yielded to their families' wishes, and He counselled them to be merciful to their families.[10]

In summary, Islam counsels moderation. In worldly concerns, unquestionably, from the perspective of the mother, her family comes first. But Allah has His due. Thus, the mother should be affectionate, generous and concerned about her family's needs, up to the point where they prevent her from participating in activities which strengthen her faith and knowledge of her religion, and at the very least, she must not become distracted from completing the obligatory duties. As Allah has given the Muslim mother the awareness that her love for her children will be a test of her faith, she must try to counteract this tendency to distraction by bringing them up in a balanced atmosphere - one in which love for family and remembrance of Allah exist side by side.

NOTES

[1]*Ṣaḥīḥ Al-Bukhārī,* v. 1, Kitāb Al-Ādhān, p. 381.

[2]Aṭ-Ṭabarī, v. 28, p. 117. Also, Al-Qurṭubī, v. 18, p. 129.

[3]Ibn Kathīr, v. 2, p. 301.

[4]*Riyāḍ Aṣ-Ṣāliḥīn,* Bāb Faḍl Al-Ḥubb Fī Allah Wa Al-Ḥathth 'Alaihi, p. 118. Also, Ibn Kathīr, op. cit.

[5]*Ṣaḥīḥ Al-Bukhārī,* v. 1, Kitāb Al-'Īmān, p. 20. Also, Ibn Kathīr, op. cit.

[6]Aṭ-Ṭabarī, v. 9, p. 224.

[7]Al-Qurṭubī, v. 18, p. 142.

[8]Ibn Kathīr, v. 4, p. 376.

[9]Al-Qurṭubī, v. 18, p. 141.

[10]Ibn Kathīr, v. 4, p. 376. Also, Aṭ-Ṭabarī, v. 28, pp. 124-125.

PART III

THE PERSPECTIVE OF FATHER AND MOTHER IN CASE OF DIVORCE

CHAPTER VII

FINANCIAL RESPONSIBILITIES AND NURSING RIGHTS

It is an accepted principle in Islam that within the context of marriage the father is fully responsible for the *nafaqah* (support) of his wife, whether she is the mother of his child or not, and whether she is rich or poor. He is also responsible for the *nafaqah* of his minor children, if they are not independently wealthy.[1] This is based on the Qur'ānic verses to be discussed below and the following Ḥadīth:

« أخبرنا سفيان عن هشام بن عروة عن أبيه عن عائشة رضى آلله عنها أن هند بنت عتبة أتت النبىّ ﷺ فقالت يارسول آلله إن أبا سفيان رجل شحيح وليس لى منه إلّا مايدخل علىّ فقال النبىّ ﷺ خذى مايكفيك وولدك بالمعروف » .

> "Narrated 'Ā'ishah (رضى) that Hind bint 'Utbah came to the Prophet (ﷺ) and she said: O Messenger of Allah, Abū Sufyān is a miserly man and I have nothing from him except what I take for myself. And the Prophet (ﷺ) said: Take what is sufficient for you and your child *bil ma'rūf* (in fairness)."[2]

However, if the mother is divorced, the father's relationship to her and the children must be defined legally. As the *nafaqah* for the mother based on matrimonial restraint is no longer operative, the father's financial contribution to her must be specified. Other areas that require legal definition are nursing rights and custody of the children.

The three following verses form the basis for legal rulings of such rights and financial obligations as pertain in cases of divorce:

> "Lodge them where ye dwell, according to your wealth, and harass them not so as to straiten life for them. And if

they are with child, then spend for them till they bring forth their burden. Then, if they give suck for you, give them their due payment and consult together in kindness; but if ye make difficulties for one another, then let some other woman give suck for him. Let him who hath abundance spend of his abundance, and he whose provision is measured, let him spend of that which Allah hath given him. Allah asketh naught of any soul save that which He hath given it." (65:6-7)

"Mothers shall suckle their children for *ḥaulain kāmilain,*[3] (that is) for those who wish to complete the suckling. The duty of feeding and clothing the nursing mother in a seemly manner is upon the father of the child. No one should be burdened beyond his capacity. A mother should not be treated unfairly because of her child, nor should he to whom the child is born (be treated unfairly) because of his child. And on the (father's) heir is incumbent the like of that (which was incumbent on the father). If they desire to wean the child by mutual consent and (after) joint consultation, it is no sin for them; and if ye wish to give your children out to nurse, it is no sin for you, provided that ye pay what is due from you in fairness." (2:233)

Based on the Qur'ānic texts, there is no disagreement amongst the *'Ulamā'* about the obligation of the father to provide support and housing for the pregnant divorced woman during the period of her *'iddah*[4] and until she gives birth, if the pregnancy continues after the period of the *'iddah.* This applies whether she is divorced in the category of *mabtūtah* (irreversibly divorced) or that of *raj'iyyah* (reversibly divorced).[5] In addition, there is agreement that the *raj'iyyah* is entitled to housing and *nafaqah* during the *'iddah,* even if she is not pregnant. The question arises about *nafaqah* during the period of the *'iddah* for the mother, divorced in the category of *mabtūtah,* who is not pregnant. The basis of the disagreement is found in the following Ḥadīth of Fāṭimah bint Qais, who had been pronounced irreversibly divorced, and 'Umar Ibn Al-

Khaṭṭāb's reply to it:

« روى عن فاطمة بنت قيس قالت طلقنى زوجى ثلاثا فلم يفرض لى رسول آلله ﷺ سكنى ولا نفقة » .

"Fāṭimah bint Qais said: My husband divorced me three times (i.e., irreversibly) and the Messenger of Allah (ﷺ) did not entitle me to either housing or *nafaqah.*"[6]

« عن حماد عن إبراهيم عن الأسود قال قال عمر بن الخطاب رضى آلله عنه : لا ندع كتاب ربنا وسنة نبينا ﷺ بقول امرأة لا ندرى صدقت أم كذبت ، المطلقة ثلاثا لها السّكنى والنفقة » .

"'Umar Ibn Al-Khaṭṭāb (رضى) said: Don't give up the Book of our Lord and the Sunnah of our Prophet (ﷺ) on (the basis of) the statement of a woman, we don't know whether she spoke the truth or lied. The woman divorced by the three pronouncements of the formula gets housing and support."[7]

Thus, according to the School of Abū Ḥanīfah and his companions, the irreversibly divorced mother, who is not pregnant, is entitled to housing and support; while the Schools of Mālik and Ash-Shāfi'ī say she is entitled to housing, but not to support, and the School of Aḥmad Ibn Ḥanbal, says that she is neither entitled to support nor to housing.[8]

The nursing period as stated in the Qur'ān is « حَوْلَيْنِ كَامِلَيْنِ » which is generally considered to be two complete years. During this period, there are three possibilities for the divorced mother: (1) that she nurses her child; (2) that she "refuses to nurse" and gives him to a wet nurse; and (3) that she and the father agree to wean the child. In reference to option number one, Mālik says « حق الرضاع لها لا عليها » i.e., the divorced mother has the right to nurse her child, but she also has a choice.[9] Qatādah puts it another way saying that the mother has more right to the child if she agrees to nurse him.[10]

If the mother nurses during the period of her *'iddah,* then the above-mentioned financial responsibilities apply. If she continues to nurse after the *'iddah,* the father must provide her with a financial reward, as *nafaqah* is only due to the pregnant divorcee after completion of the *'iddah.* In such a case, if the father says he will not provide the mother with financial compensation and hires a wet nurse, and the mother is agreeable to nursing the child for the same amount or for nothing, the mother has more right. But if the natural mother asks for more money than the wet nurse does, the father is not forced to hire the mother, as the Qur'ānic injunction is that neither parent should use the child as a means of harming the other.[11] The following Ḥadīth strongly emphasizes these points:

« قال يُونسُ عن الزهرى : نَهىَ آللهُ تعالىٰ أن تضارَّ والدة بولدها ، وذلك أن تقولَ الوالدة : لسْتُ مُرْضعتهُ وهى أمْثَل له غذاءً وأشفقُ عليه وأرفقُ به من غيرها فليس لها أن تأبَى بعد أن يعطيها من نفسه ماجَعَلَ آللهُ عليه ، وليس للمولود له أن يُضارَّ بولدِهِ والدتهُ ، فيمنعُها أن تُرضِعَهُ ضراراً لها إلى غيرها » .

> "Yūnus said on the authority of Az-Zuhrī: Allah has forbidden that a (divorced) mother should hurt her child by saying, 'I am not going to suckle it' for her milk is the best for it and she is usually kinder and more gentle to it than any other woman. Therefore, she should not refuse (to suckle) it after her husband has provided her with what Allah has enjoined upon him. And a father should not use his child to hurt its mother by preventing the latter from suckling it just to harm her by giving it to some other woman." (Al-Bukhārī)[12]

Thus, Al-Qurṭubī says that each parent should approach what Allah has commanded him (or her) to do in the best of kindness. And the best on the mother's part is the nursing of the child without financial reward. And the best on the father's part is to provide her with the financial reward for nursing.[13]

If the divorced mother "refuses to nurse" due to sickness or some other excuse, this is legally recognized only if it is within the allowed nursing period:

« قال الترمذى (باب ماجاء أن الرضاعة لا تحرم إلّا فى الصغر دون الحولين)
حدثنا قتيبة حدثنا أبو عوانه عن هشام عن عروة عن فاطمة بن المنذر عن أم سلمة
قالت : قال رسول آلله ﷺ : لا يحرم من الرضاع إلا مافتق الأمعاء فى الثدى و كان
قبل الفطام » .

"Narrated Umm Sallamah: She said: The Messenger of Allah (ﷺ) said: There is no refusing of the nursing relationship unless the unripe date (the babe) is rent from the breast and it is (during the period) before the weaning time." (Aṭ-Tirmidhī, Bāb Mā Jā'a 'An Ar-Raḍā'ah Lā Taḥram Illa Fī Aṣ-Ṣaghar Dūna Al-Ḥaulain)[14]

Aṭ-Ṭabarī comments that there is no sin on the parents if they give the child to an affectionate wet nurse, in a situation where they do not feel that the weaning of the child would be healthy for it and the mother is prevented from nursing due to her weakness, illness or some other valid excuse.[15] Ibn Kathīr adds that the mother should not relinquish the new-born infant until she has given him the first milk which flows, the drinking of which is necessary for him to survive. After that she can relinquish him if she wishes, but if it is in order to harm his father, then that is not permissible, just as it is not permissible for the father to take the child from her merely to cause harm to her.[16]

In addition, if the parents through mutual consultation agree to wean the child before the completion of *ḥaulain kāmilain,* being of the opinion that it is best for the child, there is no sin on them in doing so. It is understood by this that one of the parents making the decision singly without the other does not suffice. This requirement contains in it precautions for the child and obligations in the handling of his matter.[17] Aṭ-Ṭabarī adds, however, that although there is no sin in weaning the child, it should be kept in mind that if the child is separated from the bond that was between him and his mother through weaning, he is thereby denied both his mother's tenderness and the nourishment from her breast, nourishment which leads to the formation of the mature adult.[18]

In summary, the best situation is obviously one in which the original family members remain as one harmonious unit, each parent fulfilling his or her obligations to bring up sound, healthy children. Thus, in situations of stress, it is customary, in Islam, for members of the extended family to exert as much effort as possible to try to keep the nuclear family together. If they are not successful, however, Islam does allow for divorce. Under any circumstances, it is best for the mother to nurse her own child; consequently, Islam has given her the first right to do so, as in this case the innocent child will not be denied the nourishment and natural affection he so direly needs. If, in a divorce situation, however, it is not possible for the mother to nurse her child, she may relinquish her right and the father may then hire a wet nurse, or they may jointly decide to wean the child. Whichever course is chosen, however, it should not be based on selfish or spiteful intentions, but rather on necessity and concern for the welfare of the child.

NOTES

[1]Muḥammad Ibn Idrīs Ash-Shāfi'ī, *Kitāb Al-Umm* (Egypt: Bil Maṭba'ah Al-Kubrā Al-Amīriyyah Bi Būlāq, 1903/1322) v. 7, Kitāb An-Nafaqah, Bāb An-Nafaqah 'Alā An-Nisā', p. 95. Also, Abū Ḥanīfah further states that underlying this requisite is the fact that *nafaqah* is recompense for matrimonial restraint i.e., cohabitation rights; see, Burhān Ad-Dīn 'Alī Ibn Abī Bakr Al-Marghinānī, *Kitāb Al-Hidāyah* (Cairo: Bil Maṭba'ah Al-Khairiyyah, 1326 Heg.) v. 2, Bāb An-Nafaqah, p. 33. Also, according to Mālik, if there is no father and the child has no wealth, the mother is financially responsible for the child; see, Ḥasan Kāmil Al-Malṭāwī, *Fiqh Al-Mu'āmalāt 'Alā Madhhab Al-Imām Mālik* (Cairo: Al-Majlis Al-A'lā, 1972) p. 60.

[2]*Kitāb Al-Umm,* op. cit. Ash-Shāfi'ī also states that *bil ma'rūf* means an amount equal to the accepted standard (مثل) of the country they live in. Also, on p. 96, Bāb Al-Khilāf Fī Nafaqah Al-Mar'ah, Ash-Shāfi'ī states that if the husband does not provide the wife with *nafaqah,* while they are still married, they should be separated (i.e., divorced) based on the Prophet's (ﷺ) order to give *nafaqah* and Abū Hurairah's (رضى) statement: "Your wife says provide me with *nafaqah* or divorce me, and your slave says provide me with *nafaqah* or sell me." Also, *Al-Hidāyah,* op. cit.: Abū Ḥanīfah states that the rank and

condition of both the wife and her husband must be considered in determining what the suitable amount for *nafaqah* is, both in marriage and in divorce.

[3]*Ḥaulain kāmilain* is generally considered to be two complete years; see Aṭ-Ṭabarī, v. 2, pp. 491-493. Abū Ḥanīfah, however, considers it to be thirty months; see *Al-Hidāyah,* v. 1, Kitāb Ar-Raḍā', p. 176.

[4]The *'iddah* is the term incumbent upon a woman in consequence of dissolution of marriage after consummation, in the case of divorce or the death of the husband. It is the term, by completion of which, a new marriage is rendered legal. There are three possibilities for the *'iddah* of divorce: (1) if the woman menstruates, the *'iddah* is three courses; (2) if she does not menstruate, the *'iddah* is three months; (3) if she is pregnant, the *'iddah* continues until delivery. See, *Al-Hidāyah,* v. 2, Bāb Al-'Iddah, p. 23. Also, *nafaqah* is not due during the *'iddah* when separation originates with the woman due to a crime, e.g., apostasy, because this is as if she had left her husband's house recalcitrantly. *Nafaqah* is due if she separates herself because of a just demand. See, *Al-Hidāyah,* v. 2, Bāb An-Nafaqah, pp. 37-38. Also, *nafaqah* does not apply to wives who did not live with their husbands. See, Al-Qurṭubī, v. 18, p. 166.

[5]Al-Qurṭubī, v. 18, p. 168.

[6]*Al-Hidāyah,* v. 2, op. cit. Also, Al-Qurṭubī, v. 18, p. 167.

[7]Abū Ḥanīfah An-Nu'mān Ibn Thābit Ibn Zuṭā' Al-Taymī, *Kitāb Al-Musnad* (Cairo: Maktabah Al-Adab, 1981) pp. 106-107. Also, Al-Qurṭubī, op. cit.

[8]This also applies to the irreversibly divorced wife, who is not a mother; see *Al-Hidāyah,* v. 2, Bāb An-Nafaqah, pp. 37-38; *Kitāb Al-Umm* (in the margin), v. 5, Nafaqah Allatī La Yamliku Zaujuha Raji'atuha Wa Ghairu Dhālika, p. 79; Al-Qurṭubī, v. 18, p. 167. Also, Ibn Kathīr concurs with Abū Ḥanīfah's opinion, saying that the verses (65:6-7) refer to irreversibly divorced wives and not to the *raj'iyyah,* as the reversibly divorced wife obviously gets housing and support anyway, and that pregnant ex-wives are specified in the Qur'ānic text in order to include a period possibly longer than the *'iddah*; see Ibn Kathīr, v. 4, p. 383. Aṭ-Ṭabarī holds with the opinion of Mālik and Ash-Shāfi'ī; see v. 18, p. 147. Al-Qurtubī's opinion agrees with that of Aḥmad; see, v. 3, p. 160.

[9]Al-Malṭāwī, p. 58.

[10]Aṭ-Ṭabarī, v. 2, p. 497.

[11]*Al-Hidāyah,* v. 2, Bāb An-Nafaqah, p. 38. Also, Al-Malṭāwī, p. 58. Also, during the *'iddah,* the financial reward is due to the nursing *mabtūtah* according to the Schools which do not provide her with *nafaqah.*

[12]*Ṣaḥiḥ Al-Bukhārī,* v. 7, Kitāb An-Nafaqah, p. 209.

[13]Al-Qurṭubī, v. 18, p. 169. Also, according to Aṭ-Ṭabarī, Ja'far, Abū Ḥanīfah, Qatādah and Al-Ḥasan, if the father dies, the child-heir is responsible for the financial reward. Al-Qurṭubī, Mālik, Ash-Shāfi'ī, Az-Zuhrī and Aḍ-Ḍaḥḥāk say that the child-heir is not responsible for the financial reward; see Al-Qurṭubī, v. 3, pp. 166-168 and Aṭ-Ṭabarī, v. 2, p. 505.

[14]Ibn Kathīr, v. 1, p. 283.

[15]Aṭ-Ṭabarī, v. 2, p. 509. He adds that the father is responsible for paying the wet nurse the financial reward that was agreed upon at the time of the contract of hiring. Also according to Mālik if the father is impoverished and has no wealth for the child, the mother has to nurse him, and if she does not have milk and has wealth, then the nursing of the child is her responsibility from her wealth; see Al-Qurṭubī, v. 3, p. 161 and Al-Malṭāwī, p. 58.

[16]Ibn Kathīr, v. 1, p. 284.

[17]Ibid.

[18]Aṭ-Ṭabarī, v. 2, pp. 505-506.

CHAPTER VIII

CUSTODY OF THE CHILD

The decision as to which parent will receive custody of the child is determined in Islam by reference to the Sunnah of the Prophet (ﷺ), analogy and reference to juridical rulings. In all of these cases, the circumstances involved are taken into consideration. The key underlying factors are the strong natural bond that exists between mother and child, and the child's right to choose when he or she is of age to do so. This is balanced with the necessity of satisfying certain inevitable needs of the child. The following Ḥadīth indicates the great importance given to the mother-child relationship:

« عن أبى أيوب قال : سمعت رسول آلله ﷺ يقول : من فرق بين والدة وولدها فرق آلله بينه وبين أحبته يوم القيامة » .

> "Narrated Abū Ayyūb: I heard the Messenger of Allah (ﷺ) say: Whoever separates the mother and child, Allah will separate him and his most beloved (wife) on the Day of Ascension." (At-Tirmidhī and Aḥmad)[1]

Al-Qurṭubī also emphasizes the importance of the mother to the child in his statement. He says that since divorced women have more right to nurse their children because they are more affectionate and more gentle, and taking the small child away from his mother is harmful to both of them, this points to the fact that the mother continues to have more right to raise him after the age of weaning, due to her kindness and tenderness; however, he adds, she has more right to raise him if she does not re-marry.[2]

The legal decisions about child custody have been based primarily on the three following Ḥadīths:

« حدثنا محمد بن خالد السّلمى حدثنا الوليد عن أبى عمرو يعنى الأوزاعى حدثنا

عمرو بن شعيب عن أبيه عن جده عبد آلله بن عمرو أن امرأة قالت يارسول آلله ابنى هذا كان بطنى له وعاء وثديى له سقاء وحجرى له حواء وإن أباه طلقنى وأراد أن ينتزعه منى فقال لها رسول آلله ﷺ أنتِ أحق به مالم تنكحى » .

"'Amr Ibn Shu'aib reported that his father said that his grandfather said: A woman came to the Prophet (ﷺ) and said: O Messenger of Allah, I have been divorced from my husband and he wants to take this son of mine from me. But my stomach was a dwelling for him, my breast a source of nourishment for him; and my lap a resting place for him. And now he wants to snatch him away from me! The Prophet said: No. You have more right to him unless you re-marry." (Abū Dāwūd, Aḥmad, Al-Baihaqī and Al-Ḥākim)[3]

« عن أبى هريرة أن النبى ﷺ خيّر غلاماً بين أبيه وأمه فأخذ بيدها فانطلقت به» .

"On the authority of Abū Hurairah that the Prophet (ﷺ) gave a boy a chance to choose between his father and his mother. And the boy took his mother's hand and she left with him." (At-Tirmidhī, An-Nasā'ī, Ibn Mājah and Al-Ḥākim)[4]

« ذكر عبد الرزاق عن ابن جريج أنه أخبره عن عطاء الخراسانى عن ابن عباس قال : طلق عمر بن الخطاب امرأته الأنصارية أم ابنه عاصم ولقيها تحمله بمحسّر وقد فطم ومشى فأخذ بيده لينزعه منها ونازعها اياه حتّى أوجع الغلام وبكى وقال أنا أحق بابنى منك فاختصما إلى أبى بكر فقضى لها به وقال ريحها وفراشها وحرها خير له منك حتّى يشب ويختار لنفسه ، وذكر عن الثورى عن عاصم عن عكرمة قال خاصمت امرأة عمر إلى أبى بكر رضى آلله عنه وكان طلقها فقال أبو بكر الأم أعطف وألطف وأرحم وأحنى وأخير وأرأف وهى أحق بولدها مالم تتزوج » .

"Ibn 'Abbās reported: 'Umar Ibn Al-Khaṭṭāb divorced his Anṣārī wife, the mother of his son 'Āṣim. And he met her carrying him in an impoverished state. He had been weaned by that time. So he took him by the hand, pulling him from her, and she, pulling him towards her until the boy was hurt and started to cry. And he said: I am more entitled to him than you are. Disputing, they went to Abū Bakr who decreed that she should have the boy, saying: Her fragrance and her comforting warmth is better for him than you are, until he becomes older and is able to decide for himself. "And in another narration, Abū Bakr said: "The mother is more affectionate, kinder, more compassionate, more loving, much better, more gracious and she is more entitled to her child as long as she does not re-marry." ('Abd Ar-Razzāq)[5]

In Ibn Al-Qayyim's discussion of "the mother has more right to the child", he refers to the three above-mentioned Ḥadīths, then he cites other judgements made by the Companions in favour of the mother, which indicate that the child should be allowed to choose when he is of age to do so:

« ذكر عبد الرزاق عن معمر عن أيوب عن إسماعيل بن عبد آلله عن عبد الرحمٰن بن غنم قال اختصم إلى عمر بن الخطاب رضى آلله عنه فى غلام فقال هو مع أمه حتى تُعرِبَ عنه لسانه فيختَارَ » .

"Ismā'īl Ibn 'Abdullah said 'Abd Ar-Raḥmān Ibn Ghunam said: A dispute was brought to 'Umar Ibn Al-Khaṭṭāb (رضى) regarding a boy. He said: He remains with his mother until he is able to express himself clearly in order to choose (between his parents)." ('Abd Ar-Razzāq)[6]

« ذكر سعيد بن منصور عن هشام عن خالد عن الوليد بن مسلم قال اختصموا إلى عمر بن الخطاب رضى آلله عنه فى يتيم فخيره فأختار أمه على عمه فقال عمر رضى آلله عنه إن لطف أمك خير من خصب عمك » .

"Al-Walīd Ibn Muslim said: A dispute was brought to 'Umar Ibn Al-Khaṭṭāb (رضى) regarding an orphan. The child was asked to choose, and he chose his mother instead of his paternal uncle. And 'Umar said: Indeed, the gentleness of your mother is better than the abundance (of wealth) of your uncle."[7]

« قال الشافعي رحمه آلله تعالى أنبأنا سفيان بن عيينة عن يونس بن عبد آلله الجرمي عن عمارة الجرمي قال خيرني عليّ رضي آلله عنه بين أمي وعمي ثم قال لأخ لي أصغر مني وهذا أيضا لو قد بلغ مبلغ هذا لخيرته » .

"According to Sufyān Ibn 'Uyainah, 'Imārah Al-Jaramī said: 'Alī (رضي) made me choose between my mother and my paternal uncle. He then said to my brother younger than I. And this one too. Had he been as old as this one, I would have made him choose too." (Ash-Shāfi'ī)[8]

In the period of infancy before the child is able to choose, the *'Ulamā'* agree that it stays with the mother, even if she is a non-Muslim. In the case of the non-Muslim mother, however, once the child reaches the age at which he is capable of forming judgement with respect to religion, he goes to the Muslim father, and if the mother indicates that she is bent on bringing up the child as a non-Muslim, she will not be given the child in any case.[9]

Although the Ḥadīths indicate "choosing", Ibn Al-Qayyim notes that there are disputes amongst the *'Ulamā'* about these Ḥadīths and consequently about the requirement of choosing, especially with respect to the girl, as the children mentioned in the Ḥadīths were boys. Thus, some have concluded that a girl should not choose, but should be placed in either the mother's home or the father's. Imām Mālik, Imām Abū Ḥanīfah, and also Imām Aḥmad, in one narration about him, say that the girl should be placed with the mother. Ibn Al-Qayyim concurs with this opinion because the natural mother is the person most concerned about her daughter's virtue and her education, while her father, having to work outside the home, is not able to attend to either. He says, however, that the best-known opinion of the Ḥanbalī School is that the girl should stay with the father, as he is more solicitous of her virtue and can better look after her interests with respect to marriage arrangements and the like.[10]

The following is a summary of the conclusions of the Four Schools with reference to the age at which children, in case of divorce, should either be separated from their mothers and put in the custody of their fathers, or should be allowed to choose. Ash-Shāfi'ī says that the child (boy or girl) stays with the mother until it is seven or eight years old, and then chooses. He said the child chooses at this age because he has reached the stage where he is mature enough to be actively interested in learning the Qur'ān, manners and the responsibilities of religious duties of worship; and the boy and the girl are equal. Ash-Shāfi'ī adds that whichever parent is chosen, that parent has no right to forbid the other from visiting the child.[11] Abū Ḥanīfah says the mother has more right to the girl until she menstruates, and to the boy until he can eat and drink by himself and dress himself, i.e., around seven years of age; then the children go to the father. He does not consider "choosing" as an alternative.[12] There are different opinions within the Mālikī School, but the most prevalent one seems to be that the boy stays with the mother until « احتلامه » (around the age of puberty), and the girl until marriage which is consummated. Some of the Mālikī *'Ulamā'* allow choosing and others do not.[13] Ibn Ḥanbal's preferred opinion is in agreement with that of Ash-Shāfi'ī, that the child (boy or girl) stays with the mother until seven years of age, and then chooses, but the Ḥanbalī School also allows for the possibility of a girl staying with her mother until she is nine years old, and then going to the father.[14] Thus, all of the Schools agree that in case of divorce the mother has more right to the child for the first seven years of its life, and then the daughter is either given the right to choose or is placed with the mother until she reaches a marriageable age, at which time it is felt that her best interests lie with her father. With the boy however, Abū Ḥanīfah feels that his best interests will be served by placing him with the father at an early age, while the other Schools see his situation to be more or less the same as that of the daughter.

The decision as to which parent should be the guardian is also based on whether or not this person will bring up the child in a correct and Islamic environment. Accordingly, Ibn Al-

Qayyim heard his *shaikh,* Aḥmad Ibn Ḥanbal, describe a case in which a father and mother were disputing over their son before the judges. They let the boy choose, and he chose his father. So, the mother asked him why he had done so, and the boy said that his mother had always sent him to the *Kuttāb* (Qur'ān school), and the teachers punished him, while his father would let him play with the other boys. The judge gave the boy to his mother saying she had more right to him. Thus, Aḥmad Ibn Ḥanbal said that a parent has not done his duty as a guardian, if he (or she) does not instil in the child the necessity of obedience to Allah and His Prophet (ﷺ) as best he can.[15]

Ibn Al-Qayyim concludes that both parents have responsibilities to the child, the father's is financial and the mother's is to bring the child up "purely" (of sound health and spirit). The priority of the mother, he states, in nursing and early child rearing[16] comes from her care for the children, and her attentiveness to them, her friendliness and her patience at the task. Ibn Al-Qayyim goes on to say that in reference to divorced mothers who do re-marry, the Prophet (ﷺ) did not categorically deny them the right to bring up their children, for, he says, how could the child be better off being brought up by a strange woman, especially when it is the mother who, as previously stated, has more right to him.[17]

Finally returning once more to the basic source for the great respect for and rights due to the mother, that of her exhausting effort in childbirth, Ibn Quṭaibah includes a Ḥadīth which indicates that it is also a reason for her priority in child-rearing – to such a degree that the father has to acknowledge the mother's right:

« خاصمت أمّ عوفٍ امرأة أبى الأسود الدؤليّ أبا الأسود إلى زياد فى ولدها منه : قال أبو الأسود : أنا أحقُّ بالولد منها ، حملتُه قبل أن تحمله ، ووضعتُه قبل أن تضعه ، فقالت أمُّ عوفٍ : وضعته شهوةً ووضعتُه كُرهاً ، وحملتَه خِفاً وحملتهُ ثقلًا ، فقال زياد : صدقتِ ، أنتِ أحق به ، فدفعه إليها » .

"Umm 'Awf, the wife of Abū Al-Aswad Ad-Du'lī, brought a legal dispute against Abū Al-Aswad to Ziyād in the case of her child from him. Abū Al-Aswad said: I have more right to the child than she does. I bore the burden of it (financially) before she bore the burden of it (in pregnancy); and I unburdened myself of it (produced it) before she unburdened herself of it (gave birth to it). Then, Umm 'Awf said: You produced it ardently (desiringly) while I gave birth to it against my will (despisedly). And your burden with it was light (easy), while mine was heavy (difficult). So, Ziyād said: You have spoken the truth. You are more entitled to him. And he handed the child over to her."[18]

In summary, as child custody, in the case of divorce, is not based on Qur'ānic injunction, there is variance of opinion about the matter. There is universal acceptance of the principle that the mother has more right to rear the child, based on her great capacity for affection and concern for him. The *'Ulamā'* disagree, however, about which age is appropriate or necessary for the father to assume guardianship of the child. Furthermore, the mother's right may be tempered by other factors, such as the child's independent choice, or the choice of the judge based on moral or other considerations. In addition, if the mother remarries outside the paternal family or leaves the country, she may lose her automatic right to rear the child. Thus, the *'Ulamā'* have tried to formulate rulings that will make the best of a difficult situation. All of these rulings, however varying they may be, are made in an attempt to provide the child with the best environment, one which satisfies the different needs he has at different stages of his development. It is obvious, however, that in the case of a broken family, no solution is perfectly suitable, especially for the children. This, itself, should be a precaution against divorce, as nothing can substitute for the necessary input of both father and mother towards the rearing of balanced, mature and – from the point of view of Islam – pious adults.

NOTES

[1]Khān, Bāb Mā Warada Fī Tafrīq Al-Walad 'An Al-Wālidah, p. 241.

[2]Al-Qurṭubī, v. 3, p. 160.

[3]*Sunan Abū Dāwūd,* v. 1, Kitāb An-Nikāḥ, Bāb Man Aḥaqqu Bi Al-Walad, p. 277. Also, Khān, Bāb Mā Warada Fī Al-Ḥaḍānah, p. 280.

[4]Khān, op. cit. Also, *Kanz,* v. 5, p. 573 (No. 14009). Also, *Kitāb Al-Umm,* v. 5, Bāb Ayyi Al-Wālidain Aḥaqqu Bi Al-Walad, p. 82. Also, *Al-Hidāyah,* v. 2, Bāb Al-Walad Wa Man Aḥaqqu Bihi, p. 31.

[5]Al-Imām Shams Ad-Dīn Ibn 'Abdullah Ibn Al-Qayyim, *Kitāb Zādu Al-Ma'ād Fī Hudan Khair Al-'Ibād* (Cairo: Maṭba'ah Muṣṭafā Al-Bāna Al-Ḥalabī, 1971/1391) v. 4, p. 151. Also, *Kanz,* v. 5, p. 576 (No. 14020).

[6]*Zādu Al-Ma'ād,* v. 4, p. 164. Also, *Kanz,* v. 5, p. 577 (No. 14026).

[7]*Zādu Al-Ma'ād,* op. cit.

[8]Ibid., v. 4, p. 150. Also, *Kitāb Al-Umm* (In the margin), v. 5, Bāb Ayyi Al-Wālidain Aḥaqqu Bi Al-Walad, pp. 83-84.

[9]*Al-Hidāyah,* v. 2, Bāb Al-Walad Wa Man Aḥaqqu Bihi, p. 32. Also, *Zādu Al-Ma'ād,* v. 4, pp. 161-162.

[10]*Zādu Al-Ma'ād,* v. 4, p. 168.

[11]*Kitāb Al-Umm,* v. 5, Bāb Ayyi Al-Wālidain Aḥaqqu Bi Al-Walad, p. 82, and (in the margin), p. 84. Also, Al-Qurṭubī, v. 3, p. 164.

[12]*Al-Hidāyah,* v. 2, Bāb Al-Walad Wa Man Aḥaqqu Bihi, p. 32.

[13]Al-Malṭāwī, p. 61. Also, Al-Qurṭubī, v. 3, p. 164. Also, see *Zādu Al-Ma'ād,* v. 4, pp. 165-166 for the difference of opinion within the Mālikī School.

[14]*Zādu Al-Ma'ād,* op. cit.

[15]*Zādu Al-Ma'ād,* v. 4, p. 169.

[16]The mother has more right only if she continues to live in the same country as the father, and if she does not re-marry, unless she marries a relative of the father. If she does marry outside the family, and this marriage is subsequently dissolved, her right to the child returns to her, as the obstruction to it no longer exists; see *Al-Hidāyah,* v. 2, p. 32 and *Kitāb Al-Umm,* v. 5, p. 82.

[17]*Zādu Al-Ma'ād,* v. 4, p. 163. Also, see Al-Qurṭubī, v. 3, p. 165. Ibn Al-Mandhur reported that the judge, 'Abd Al-Wahhāb in his commentary on Al-Ḥasan said that the mother's right to rear her child is not abolished by the re-marriage.

[18]Abū Muḥammad 'Abdullah Ibn Muslim Ibn Qutaibah Ad-Dinawrī, *'Uyyūn Al-Akhbār* (Egypt: Dār Al-Kutub), v. 4, Kitāb An-Nisā', Bāb Al-Wālidah Wa Al-Walad, p. 122.

PART IV

CONCLUSION

CHAPTER IX

THE MUSLIMAH AS BELIEVER, WIFE AND MOTHER

The natural order of relationships in Islam is hierarchical. It might be described visually as a step-pyramid, split from top to bottom into two halves. One half represents wordly concerns, and the other half spiritual concerns. Allah in His Perfection exists above the pyramid, and it is to His will and judgement that all His creatures are subject. The hierarchical relationships in the worldly sphere exist to keep order in this life. In this context, equality exists only within status bars, i.e., for those on the same step of the pyramid. Thus, Muslims are counselled to treat their children equally, to treat wives equally, etc. Total equality is a concept which exists only in relationship to just rewards, good or bad, in the Hereafter, for deeds accomplished during one's lifetime. Consequently, the Muslim woman lives her worldly life, willing to sacrifice personal desire, in the hope that she will arrive at the top of the spiritual half of the pyramid. She tries to fulfil her daily responsibilities as best she can, seeking Allah's mercy and blessings.

Relationships in this world are hierarchical while at the same time they are interdependent. Just as the pyramid would crumble if one of its steps was removed, so it becomes stronger if each step supports the other. Thus, the Muslimah is responsible as wife to her husband, and receives her spiritual rewards as such, and at the same time, her children are responsible to her as mother, and receive their spiritual rewards as such, as indicated by the following Ḥadīth:

« عن عائشة رضى آلله عنها : أعظم الناس حقاً على المرأة زوجها ، وأعظم الناس حقاً على الرجل أمّه» .

"Narrated 'Ā'ishah (رضى) : The person who has the greatest right over the woman is her husband, and the

> person who has the greatest right over the man is his mother." (Al-Ḥākim in *Al-Mustadrak*; Al-Bazār)[1]

The cement which holds the pyramid together and gives it strength is faith and active striving to complete that which Allah has made incumbent upon the believers. In this respect, the Muslimah is held independently responsible for her acts. The Qur'ān states:

> "And whoever does deeds of righteousness – be he male or female – and he is a believer ; those will enter Paradise, and not the least injustice will be done to them." (4:124)

> "Lo! I cause not the work of any worker, male or female, to be lost." (3:195)

She is independently responsible for doing good deeds and is to be independently punished for evil deeds. The Qur'ān provides examples of the wives of the Prophets Nūḥ (ﷺ) and Lūṭ (ﷺ), women who were called to account for their evil deeds, and the opposite example of the wife of Pharaoh, known as Āsiyah, who separated herself from the misdeeds of her husband and prayed for Allah's mercy.[2]

Khadījah (رضى) the first wife of the Prophet (ﷺ) provides an exemplary model of the Muslimah as believer, wife and mother. The following Ḥadīths clearly indicate the great appreciation and respect the Prophet (ﷺ) had for her for each of her three worldly roles, and the immense spiritual reward due her:

(From a longer Ḥadīth):

« وآلله ما أبدلنى خيراً منها ، آمنت بى حين كفر الناس ، وصدقتنى إذ كذبنى الناس ، وآستنى بمالها إذ حرمنى الناس ، ورزقنى منها آلله الولد دون غيرها من النساء » .

> "And Allah did not replace for me better than she (Khadījah). She had faith in me when everyone else disbelieved in me. She believed in me when the people belied me. She shared her wealth with me when the people

rejected me. And Allah provided me with child from no other woman except her." (Ibn 'Abd Al-Birr)[3]

« حدثنا عُمَرُ بن محمد بن حسن : حدثنا أبي : حدثنا حفصٌ عن هشام عن أبيه ، عن عائشة رضى آلله عنها قالت : ما غِرْتُ على أحد من نساء النبىّ ﷺ ما غِرْتُ على خديجة وما رأيتها ، ولكن النبىّ ﷺ يكثر ذكرها ورُبّما ذبح الشاة ثمّ يقطعها أعضاءً ثمّ يبعثها فى صدائق خديجة . فربّما قلتُ له : كأنه لم يكن فى الدنيا امرأةٌ إلا خديجة ، فيقول إنها كانت وكانت وكان لى منها ولدٌ » .

"Narrated 'Ā'ishah (رضى): I did not feel jealous of any of the wives of the Prophet (ﷺ) as much as I did of Khadījah though I did not see her, but the Prophet (ﷺ) used to mention her very often, and whenever he slaughtered a sheep, he would cut its parts and send them to the women friends of Khadījah. When I sometimes said to him: It is as if there is no woman on earth except Khadījah. Then, he would say that she was this and that and from her I had child." (Al-Bukhārī, Muslim and At-Tirmidhī)[4]

« حدثنا أبو بكر بن أبى شيبة حدثنا عبد آلله بن نمير وأبو أسامة ح وحدثنا أبو كُرَيْب حدثنا أبو أُسامة وابن نميرو وكيع وأبو معاوية ح وحدثنا إسحق بن إبراهيم أخبرنا عَبْدَةُ بن سليمان كلّهم عن هشام بن عروة واللفظ حديث أبى أسامة – ح وحدثنا أبو كريب حدثنا أبو أسامة عن هشام عن أبيه قال سمعتُ عبد آلله بن جعفر يقول سمعتُ عليّا بالكوفة يقول سمعتُ رسول آلله ﷺ يقول خيرُ نسائها مريمُ بنت عمران وخيرُ نسائها خديجة بنت خويلد ، قال أبو كريب وأشار وكيعٌ إلى السّماءِ والأرض » .

"'Abdullah Ibn Ja'far reported that he heard 'Alī (رضى) say in Kūfah that the Messenger of Allah (ﷺ) said: The best of the women of her time was Mariam, the daughter of 'Imrān, and the best of the women of her time was Khadījah, the daughter of Khuwailid. Abū Kuraib said that Wakī' pointed towards the heavens and the earth." (Muslim, Al-Bukhārī and At-Tirmidhī)[5]

In the past, there was no need to specify the mother's role, as it was considered the outcome of a natural instinct, the supports for which were the Qur'ān and the Sunnah. The same may be said for obligations to the mother. But, as time passed these duties were no longer taken for granted and had to be codified and elaborated by the jurists. The trend has continued such that today Muslims even have to be reminded, for example, that transferring responsibilities for parents to institutions like old-age homes is forbidden in Islam, while there are living children to care for them. They have forgotten that "Paradise is at the foot of the mother", based on her exhausting efforts in the bearing and rearing of her children. And so it is with the importance of motherhood. Women, and the Muslim society as a whole, have lost awareness of the fact that Islam views successful motherhood as the perfection of the Muslimah's religion – that there is no better or healthier substitute for a mother's affection and concern for her children, as expressed in nursing them and just being there when she is needed, especially in the period from infancy up to the onset of adulthood.

The Islamic view is that everyone has his or her role in life, with its accompanying responsibilities to others. There is no "absolute" freedom and no "absolute" worldly equality. As previously stated, freedom has its limits, and equality exists within a structure of hierarchy. None of these realities, however, exist to prevent persons of aptitude, male or female, from making use of their talents, providing that they are beneficial to themselves and to society as a whole. The pursuit of useful knowledge, for example, is desirable and highly encouraged in Islam:

"My Lord! Increase me in knowledge." (20:114)

(From a longer Ḥadīth):

« العُلَماء هُمْ وَرَثَةُ الأنبياء ، ورّثوا العِلْم ، مَنْ أَخذَهُ اَخذَ بِحَظٍّ وافرٍ ، ومَنْ سَلَكَ طريقا يَطْلُبُ به عِلْما سَهَّل آللهُ لَهُ طريقاً إلى الجنّة » .

"The *'Ulamā'* are the inheritors of it from the Prophets, i.e., they transmitted knowledge. Whoever acquires

> knowledge, acquires a great fortune (i.e., is very fortunate). And whoever sets out on a path seeking knowledge in it, Allah eases a Path for him to Paradise." (Al-Bukhārī; Abū Dāwūd)[6]

But this does not mean that the pursuit of knowledge is a substitute for primary responsibilities. The great scholars of the past are cases in point. Abū Ḥanīfah, for example, whose scholarship formed the basis of one of the Four Schools of Islamic Law, was a merchant, thus enabling him to fulfil his role as provider within the context of family and society. The mother, no less than the father, has primary responsibilities to her family.

Muslim mothers have successfully pursued other activities, such as the attainment of knowledge, above and beyond the fulfilment of basic responsibilities to Allah and family. This is consistent within the purview of Islam, as the Muslim woman has traditionally been known to be scholar, merchant, craftswoman and, even in emergency situations, soldier. From the perspective of *sharī'ah,* however, these activities are secondary considerations, not incumbent upon all women, for a woman's basic role is that of wife and mother. Motherhood, in fact, is the special vehicle by which she attains respect in this life, and which ultimately leads to her just reward.

تمّ بحمد الله

NOTES

[1]*Nadwat Makānat Al-Mar'ah Fi Al-Usrat Al-Islāmiyyah,* (Cairo, 1975) pp. 451-452.

[2]See, Qur'ān (66:10-11).

[3]'Ā'ishah 'Abd Ar-Raḥmān (Bint Ash-Shāṭi'), *Nisā' An-Nabī* (Egypt: Dār Al-Ma'ārif, 1976) p. 28.

[4]*Ṣaḥīḥ Al-Bukhārī,* v. 5, Kitāb Manāqib Al-Anṣār, p. 104. Also, Khān, Bāb Mā Warada Fī Faḍā'il Nisā' Nabiyyina Al-Muṭahhirāt, p. 385.

[5]*Ṣaḥīḥ Muslim,* v. 15, Kitāb Faḍā'il As-Ṣaḥābah (رضى) Bāb Faḍā'il Khadījah, pp. 197-198. Also, Khān, op. cit., p. 386.

[6]*Ṣaḥīḥ Al-Bukhārī,* v. 1, Kitāb Al-'Ilm, p. 59. Also, *Sunan Abū Dāwūd,* v. 2, Awwal Kitāb Al-'Ilm, p. 81.

BIBLIOGRAPHY

ARABIC TEXTS

Qur'ān – (Reference to the translations of Marmaduke Pickthall and Yūsuf 'Alī).

'Abd Al-Bāqī, Muḥammad Fu'ād. *Al-Mu'jam Al-Mufahras Li Alfāẓ Al-Qur'ān Al-Karīm.* Beirut: Mu'assasah Jamāl Lin-Nashr.

'Abd Ar-Raḥmān, 'Ā'ishah (Bint Ash-Shāṭi'). *Nisā' An-Nabī.* Egypt: Dār Al-Ma'ārif, 1975.

__________. *Banāt An-Nabī.* Cairo: Dār Al-Hilāl, 1966/1385.

Abū Dāwūd As-Sijistānī, Sulaymān Ibn Al-Ash'ath. *As-Sunan.* Egypt: Maktabah Al-'Arab, 1863.

Abū Ḥanīfah At-Taymī, An-Nu'mān Ibn Thābit Ibn Zuṭā'. *Kitāb Al-Musnad.* Cairo: Maktabah Al-Adab, 1981.

Abū Yūsuf Al-Anṣārī, Ya'qūb Ibn Ibrāhīm. *Ikhtilāf Abī Ḥanīfah Wa Ibn Abī Laila.* Abū Al-Wafā Al-Afghānī, ed. Hyderabād: Maṭba'ah Al-'Irfān, 1938.

__________. *Kitāb Al-Āthār,* 1936.

Abū Zaid, Ḥikmat. *At-Tarbiyah Al-Islāmiyyah Wa Kifāḥ Al-Mar'ah Al-Jazā'iriyyah.* Cairo: Dār Aṭ-Ṭab'ah Al-Ḥadīthah.

'Alwān, 'Abdullah Nasīḥ. *Tarbiyah Al-Awlād.* Dār As-Salām, 1976/1397.

Al-'Aqqad, 'Abbās Maḥmud. *Al-Mar'ah Fī Al-Qur'ān.* Dār Al-Hilāl, 1962.

Bayham, Gamīl Muḥammad. *Al-Mar'ah Fī At-Tārīkh Wa Ash-Shar'.* Beirut, 1921/1334.

Al-Bukhārī, Al-Imām Abū 'Abdullah Muḥammad Ibn Ismā'īl. *Ṣaḥīḥ Al-Bukhārī.* Chicago, Ill.: Kazi Publ., 1979.

Darwāzah, Muḥammad 'Izzat. *Al-Mar'ah Fī Al-Qur'ān Wa As-Sunnah.* Egypt: Al-Maktabah Al-Miṣriyyah Al-Muqaddimah, 1967.

Adh-Dhahabī, Aḥmad Ibn Muḥammad. *Khulāṣat Taḥdhīb Al-Kāmil.* Egypt: Bil Maṭba'ah Al-Khairiyyah, 1322 Heg.

Fataḥ Allah, Ash-Shaikh Ḥamza. *Bākūrah Al-Kalām 'Ala Ḥuqūq An-Nisā' Fī Al-Islām.* Būlāq, Egypt: Bil-Maṭba'ah Al-Kubrā, 1890/1308.

Ghunaim, Aḥmad. *Al-Mar'ah Mundhu An-Nasha'a Baina At-Tajrīm Wa At-Takrīm.* Cairo: Al-Kailānī, 1980/1401.

Ḥasan, 'Abd Al-Bāṣit Muḥammad. *Makānat Al-Mar'ah Fī At-Tashrī' Al-Islāmī.* Egypt. Jāmi'at Al-Azhar, 1977.

Al-Ḥusainī, Abū An-Naṣr Mubashshir At-Tirāzī. *Al-Mar'ah Wa Ḥuqūquha Fī Al-Islām.* Cairo: Maṭba'ah As-Su'ādah, 1976.

Ibn 'Asākir, Al-Imām Abī Al-Qāsim 'Alī Ibn Al-Ḥasan Ibn Habat Allah. *Tārīkh Madīnat Dimashq.* Damascus: Al-Maṭba'ah Al-Hāshimiyyah, 1954.

Ibn Ḥajar Al-'Asqalānī, Aḥmad Ibn 'Alī. *Fatḥ Al-Bārī.* Al-Maktabah As-Salifiyyah.

__________. *Lisān Al-Mīzān.* Al-Hind: Bi Maṭba'ah Dā'irah Al-Ma'ārif An-Niẓāmiyyah, 1331 Heg.

__________. *Taḥdhīb At-Taḥdhīb.* 1907/1325.

Ibn Ḥusām Ad-Dīn Al-Hindī, 'Alā' Ad-Dīn 'Alī Al-Muttaqa. *Kanz Al-'Umāl*

Fī Sunan Al-Aqwāl (957 Heg.), Hyderabād: Dā'irah Al-Ma'ārif Al-'Uthmāniyyah, 1364 Heg.

Ibn Kathīr Al-Qurashī Ad-Dimashqī, Al-Imām 'Imād Ad-Dīn Abī Al-Fidā' Ismā'īl. *Tafsīr Al-Qur'ān Al-'Aẓīm.* Egypt: Dār Iḥyā' Al-Kutub Al-'Arabiyyah.

Ibn Manthūr Al-Ifrīqī Al-Miṣrī, Abī Faḍl Jamāl Ad-Dīn Muḥammad Ibn Makram. *Lisān Al-'Arab.* Beirut: Dār Ṣādir.

Ibn Qayyim Al-Jawziyyah, Al-Imām Shams Ad-Dīn Abū 'Abdullah. *Akhbār An-Nisā': Sharḥ Wa Taḥqīq.* Beirut: Dār Maktabah Al-Ḥayāt.

__________. *Kitāb Zādu Al-Ma'ād Fī Hudan Khair Al-'Ibād.* Cairo: Maṭba'ah Muṣṭafā Al-Bāna Al-Ḥalabī, 1971/1391.

__________. *Tuḥfat Al-Mawdūd Bi Aḥkām Al-Mawlūd.* Cairo: Maktabah Al-Qīmah, 1977/1397.

Ibn Quṭaibah Ad-Dinawrī, Abū Muḥammad 'Abdullah Ibn Muslim. *'Uyyūn Al-Akhbār.* Egypt: Dār Al-Kutub.

Ibn Sa'd, Muḥammad. *Aṭ-Ṭabaqāt Al-Kubrā.* Beirut: Dār Ṣādir.

Al-Jabrī, 'Abd Al-Muta'āl Muḥammad. *Al-Mar'ah Fī At-Taṣawwur Al-Islāmī.* Maktabah Wahbah, 1975.

Khān, Muḥammad Ṣiddīq Ḥasan. *Ḥusn Al-Uswah Bi Ma Thābit Min Allāh Wa Rasūlihi Fī An-Niswa.* Beirut: Mu'assasah Ar-Risālah, 1976.

Al-Marghinānī, Burhān Ad-Dīn 'Alī Ibn Abī Bakr. *Kitāb Al-Hidāyah.* Bi Al-Maṭba'ah Al-Khairiyyah, 1326 Heg.

Al-Malṭāwī, Ḥasan Kāmil. *Fiqh Al-Mu'āmalāt 'Alā Madhhab Al-Imām Mālik.* Cairo: Al-Majlis Al-A'lā Li Ash-Shu'ūn Al-Islāmiyyah, 1972.

Muslim Ibn Al-Hajjāj, Abū Al-Ḥasan. *Ṣaḥīḥ Muslim: Bi Sharḥ An-Nawawī.* Egypt, 1924.

Nadwat Makānat Al-Mar'ah Fī Al-Usrah Al-Islāmiyyah. Cairo, 1975.

An-Nawawī, Abū Zakariyya Yaḥya Sharaf. *Riyāḍ Aṣ-Ṣāliḥīn.* Beirut: Dār Al-Fikr.

__________. *Sharḥ An-Nawawī* (See *Ṣaḥīḥ Muslim*).

Al-Qurṭubī, Abū 'Abdullah Muḥammad Ibn Aḥmad Al-Ansārī. *Al-Jāmi' Li Aḥkām Al-Qur'ān.* Cairo: Dār Al-Kātib Al-'Arabī Li Aṭ-Ṭab'ah Wa An-Nashr 'An Ṭiba'ah Dār Al-Kutub Al-Miṣriyyah, 3rd printing, 1967/1387.

Rabī', Muḥammad Shihātah. *Dawr Al-Umm Fī 'Amalīyyat At-Taṭbī' Al-Ijtimā'ī.* Kulliyyat Al-Banāt Al-Islāmiyyah, 1977.

Ash-Shāfi'ī, Muḥammad Ibn Idrīs. *Kitāb Al-Umm.* Egypt: Bi Al-Maṭba'ah Al-Kubrā Al-Amīriyyah Bi Būlāq, 1903/1322.

__________. *Ar-Risālah.* Aḥmad Ibn Shākir, ed., 1940/1358.

Ash-Shawkānī, Muḥammad Ibn 'Alī Ibn Muḥammad. *Nail Al-Awṭār.* Cairo: Idārah Aṭ-Ṭab'ah Al-Munīrah, 1925.

Ash-Shaybānī, Abū 'Abdullah Muḥammad Ibn Al-Ḥasan. *Al-Jāmi' Al-Kabīr.* Abū Al-Wafā Al-Afghānī, ed., Lajnah Iḥyā' Al-Ma'ārif Al-'Uthmāniyyah, 1937.

Aṭ-Ṭabarī, Abū Ja'far Muhammad Jarīr. *Jāmi' Al-Bayān 'An Ta'wīl Aiy Al-Qur'ān.* Cairo: Muṣṭafā al-Bāna Al-Ḥalabī, 3rd printing, 1968/1388.

Tuffāḥah, Aḥmad Zākī. *Al-Mar'ah Wa Al-Islām*. Dār Al-Kitāb Al-Miṣrī, 1975.

Wensinck, A.J. and J.P. Mensing. *Al-Mu'jam Al-Mufahras Li Alfāẓ Al-Ḥadīth An-Nabawī*. Leiden: E.J. Brill, 1969.

ENGLISH TEXTS

'Abd Al-'Āṭī, Hammudah. *The Family Structure in Islam*. American Trust Publications, 1977.

'Abdul Rauf, Muhammad. *The Islamic View of Women and the Family*. New York: Robert Speller and Sons, Pub., Inc., 1977.

'Abdul Razack, Ismail and 'Abdul Jawad Al-Banna. *Women and Family in the Sunnah of the Prophet*. (Arabic text included). International Centre for Population Studies and Research. Al-Azhar: Dar Al-Kutub.

'Ali, Sayyid Ameer. *The Spirit of Islam*. London: Christophers, 1902.

'Ali, Maulana Muhammad. *The Religion of Islam*. U.A.R.: National Publications and Printing House.

Baveja, Malik Ram. *Women in Islam*. Hyderabad: Institute of Indo-Middle East Cultural Studies.

Galwash, Ahmad A. *The Religion of Islam*. Cairo: Imprimerie Misr S.A.E., 1957.

Gibb, H.A.R. et. al. ed. *The Encyclopedia of Islam*. London: Luzac & Co., 1960.

__________, and J.H. Kramers, ed. *The Shorter Encyclopedia of Islam*, 1961.

International Islamic Conference in Cairo, 1975. Centre for Population Studies and Research, Al-Azhar University, Dec., 1975.

Lemu, Aisha B. and Fatima Hereen. *Woman in Islam*. England: Derbyshire Print, 1976/1396.

Nasr, Seyyed Hossein. "The Male and Female in the Islamic Perspective", *Studies in Comparative Religion*. vol. xiv: 1 & 2 (Winter-Spring, 1980), pp. 67-75.

Raffel, Mindy. "The Realization of the Islamic Self", unpub. thesis. Cairo: A.U.C., 1979.

Roberts, Robert. *The Social Laws of the Qur'ān*. London: Williams and Norgate, Ltd., 1925.

Salih, Saniya 'Abd Al-Wahab. *Women in Islam: Comments and Clarifications*. Paper presented at the Univ. of Calif. in San Francisco, 1975.

Siddiqi, Dr. Muhammad Zubayr. *Ḥadīth Literature*. Calcutta: Calcutta Univ. Press, 1961.

INDEX

A

B

C

charity: [See *zakāt, ṣadaqah, waqf*]
childbirth: Intro. cf 3, 1, 2, 8, 47, Chap. V, 80, 81
child:
  custody: Chap. VIII
  equal treatment: 55, 57, 58, Chap. V cf 24, 85
  rearing: 8, 9, 21, 47, 50, Chap. V, 80, 81
choosing: 77, 78, 81
Christians: 15, 16, 27, 31, 32, 37, 40, 44, 78
companionship: 8, 25, 55

D

Aḍ-Ḍaḥḥāk: 61, Chap. VII cf 13
Ad-Dārqaṭanī: 27
death: Intro. cf 4, 12, 24-27, 53-55 [See: inheritance]
debt: 27
divorce: Chap. VII and Chap. VIII
du'ā': [See: prayer]

F

fasting: 31
Fāṭimah bint Qais: 69
financial support: [See: *nafaqah*]
fiqh: 1, 3 [See: legal requirements]
fitnah: 69-71

G

Ghunaim, Aḥmad: 1-2, Chap. V cf 9

H

Al-Ḥaddāj: 20
ḥajj: 11, 61
Al-Ḥākim: 7, 23, 26, 48, 55, 56, 76, 86
Ḥamnah bint Abī Sufyān: 40
Ḥanbal: [See: Ibn Ḥanbal]
Ḥanīfa: [See: Abū Ḥanīfah]
Al-Ḥārith: 62
Al-Ḥasan Al-Baṣrī: 9, 41, 43, 54, 56, Chap. VII cf 13, Chap. VIII cf 17
ḥaulain kāmilain: 68, 69, 71, Chap. VII cf 3
Hell: 7, 12, 19, 22-23, 27, 43, 53, 56, 62
hijrah: 23, 54, 63
ḥirmān: 34, 37

I

marriage: 51, 60, 75-76, 79-80, Chap. VIII cf 17
contract: 34
martyr: 1-2, 54
Mary: [See: Mariam (ص)]
Mazanī: 43
menstruation: 79
Moses: [See: Mūsā (ص)]
mother:
characteristics of: Chap. IV
obedience to: Chap I - Chap III
reverence to: Chap I
Al-Mughīrah: 24
Al-Muḥāmalī: 16
Al-Muḥāsibī: 21
Mujāhid: 17, 54, Chap V cf 24
Mūsā (ص): 18
Muslim: 3, 8, 10, 11, 13, 16, 18, 23–25, 47–49, 54, 57, Chap. V cf 23, 62, 87

N

nafaqah: Chap. VII, Chap. VII cf 1, 80
An-Nakha'ī: 43
An-Nasā'ī: 7, 11, 18, 23, 76
An-Nawawī: 18, 20, 23, Chap. V cf 10, cf 24
Noah: [See: Nūḥ (ص)]
Nūḥ (ص): 86
An-Nu'mān Ibn Bashīr: 57
nursing: 8, Chap. V, 80
rights: Chap. VII, 88

O

old-age: 16, 17, 18, 19, 21, 23, 88

P

Paradise: 7, 19, 23, 53, 54, 56, 58, 85
polytheists: 16, 25-27, 31-32, Chap. II cf 3, 37, 40, 44, 78
prayer: 11, 24-27, 36, 40, 51-52, 57, 60, 61
pregnancy: 8, Chap. V, 81
puberty: 79

Q

Al-Qāṣim: 17, 20
Al-Qatādah: 32–33, 41, 52, 69, Chap. VII cf 13
Quraish: 16